HARD LESSONS

Carol Ascher ◆ Norm Fruchter ◆ Robert Berne

HARD LESSONS

Public Schools and Privatization

A TWENTIETH CENTURY FUND REPORT

1996 ◆ The Twentieth Century Fund Press ◆ New York

Library of Congress Cataloging-in-Publication Data
Ascher, Carol
 Hard Lessons: the false promise of school privatization / Carol
Ascher, Norman Fruchter, Robert Berne.
   p. cm.
   "Twentieth Century Fund report."
   Includes index.
   ISBN 0-87078-399-8
   1. Privatization in education--United States.   2. Educational
vouchers--United States.   3. School choice--United States.
I. Fruchter, Norm.   II. Berne, Robert.   III. Title.
LB2806.36. A73   1996
379.3'0973--dc20   96–32848
                                                            CIP

Cover design and illustration: Claude Goodwin
Manufactured in the United States of America.

FOREWORD

Studies show that the vast majority of parents are happy with their public schools and that the number who feel that way has been growing. Still, political debate and most publicity about the nation's public schools routinely feature words like "failure, decline, and crisis." Perhaps this alarmism is a result of the media's usual focus on large, urban school districts, where educational attainment falls far below the national average. Indeed, the severity of the problems that plague the nation's most densely populated and poorest communities, combined with the difficulty of persuading voters to support expenditures for social programs, has created a new willingness among public officials, parents, and citizens in general to consider departures from established educational practices.

While there is undeniable evidence that highly targeted and very large additions to current education expenditures would enhance the education of poor children, the political realities of the 1990s make such a remedy a nonstarter. Innovations involving organizational and management changes seem especially attractive since, by contrast, they usually are described as involving lower, or even no, increases in spending. Thus, advocates of such ideas as vouchers, choice, privatization, charter schools, and a variety of other current proposals for changes in public education have found an interested audience all across the political spectrum.

One of these ideas, privatization, has the great advantage of conforming to the overwhelming popular belief that markets invariably produce better results than do governmental entities. This popular support for the concept of privatization has been a major factor underlying the willingness of local officials to consider making changes involving dismantling or superseding existing public education structures. The purists among privatizers urge these leaders to go as far as possible in the direction of producing a "true" market for education. In effect, they ask a simple question: Why not let parents buy their own education for their children? But doing so would ignore or dismiss the stake that all citizens, whether or not they have children in school, have in an educated populace.

Education is a prerequisite for a working democratic and capitalist society. Public education conveys many of the values and skills that are critical to a functional democratic political system, and an educated population is necessary for economic success. Moreover, since the benefits of an educated populace accrue to all, shouldn't the costs be borne by all? If so, education uniquely justifies the pooling of community resources. And the "profit" from our taxes invested in education is shared in the overall economic output of an advanced, rather than a third world, society. Thus, like many public services, education is a public responsibility precisely because the "profits" it produces, the fruits of an advanced industrialized nation, cannot be captured by a private proprietor.

Of course, the economics of big-city schools makes it impossible for anyone operating on a purely private basis even to hope to realize a return that would come close to justifying the necessary investment. Not surprisingly, then, most current privatization plans expect funding to continue to come entirely from public tax dollars. Cities are asked to delegate or "contract out" a governmental function to a private concern working for a profit. The notion that this approach can lead to no-cost improvement in urban schools is attractive enough to be included in the campaign appeals of many of those seeking office at all levels.

In light of the apparent popularity of this sort of privatization, it is surprising how little empirical evidence has been brought forward to support any of the schemes proposed. Surely, it cannot be the case that the actual performance of schools during previous experiments with private management is irrelevant to pending decisions. Therefore, in an effort to shed additional light on this topic, the Twentieth Century Fund asked Carol Ascher, Robert Berne, and Norm Fruchter to report on the history of privatization experiments. The authors bring considerable expertise to the task of examining what the actual experience has been with privatization around the country. Their report is comprehensive and balanced. Still, it is likely to be controversial because, based on their research, any objective observer probably would come to the conclusion that privatization is, at a minimum, being oversold. In fact, it is fair to say that there simply are no empirical results to date that would prove the promise of private management of public schools. This report, then, despite its strong grounding in the facts, is sure to be disputed by those who have a strong attachment to the notion that privatizing always improves output and by those with a financial stake in the school "industry." But, until and unless evidence to the contrary is available, any deep convictions or strong rhetoric asserted on behalf of privatization must be considered only wishful thinking.

The Twentieth Century Fund has a long history of activity related to public education and economic issues. Four years ago, we established a Task Force on School Governance; its Report, *Facing the Challenge*, made useful recommendations about the role of school boards. Earlier, we supported a Task Force to look at education in the 1980s—*Making the Grade*. This paper is the second in a series of reports the Fund is currently sponsoring on the subject of privatization; the first, *Privatization and Public Hospitals*, focused on New York City's hospitals.

In the pages that follow, the authors provide ample evidence that privatization is no magic wand that will cure the ills of the nation's urban school districts. But they are far from concluding that nothing should be done. The reason to continue to work for big-city school reform is that we cannot afford not to—not to keep asking hard questions, trying new solutions, and testing the case for greater resources. In a modern industrialized society, any time significant resources are underutilized the cost is high. In the United States, where income and wealth inequality are growing, the continuation of this pattern is also unhealthy for democracy and unity.

RICHARD C. LEONE, PRESIDENT
The Twentieth Century Fund
September 1996

CONTENTS

FOREWORD BY **RICHARD C. LEONE**   v

ACKNOWLEDGMENTS   xi

1. OUR BESIEGED PUBLIC SCHOOLS AND WHY THEY ARE PUBLIC   1

2. THE PROMISES OF PRIVATIZATION   13

3. TWO FORGOTTEN EXPERIMENTS IN SCHOOL PRIVATIZATION:
   PERFORMANCE CONTRACTING AND EDUCATIONAL VOUCHERS   23

4. PRIVATIZATION IN BALTIMORE, 1992–95   43

5. EXPERIMENTING WITH PRIVATIZATION   61

6. PUBLIC EDUCATION IN TRANSITION   83

7. THE LIMITS OF PRIVATIZATION AND THE CONTINUING
   STRUGGLE FOR EQUITY   99

NOTES   115

INDEX   135

ABOUT THE AUTHORS   143

ACKNOWLEDGMENTS

This manuscript would not have been possible without the generous support of the Twentieth Century Fund; in particular, we thank David Smith and Greg Anrig for their patience and thoughtful comments over the long course of the manuscript's development. We are also grateful to Steven Greenfield for a meticulous edit that clarified the monograph in many areas. Beverly Goldberg was a wise, energetic, and generous shepherd during the production phases.

In addition, the authors thank the Spencer Foundation, whose grant made possible the research on performance contracting, the large-scale experiment with privatization during the 1970s, described in Chapter 3.

Several individuals in and outside the Institute for Education and Social Policy at New York University assisted in the endless search for documents and reference checking necessary to the preparation of this monograph: Jody Paroff, Robert Pittenger, and Jennifer Schaeffer. As always, Gerri Pompey's loyal and friendly assistance facilitated every step.

Finally, we thank the public school families, teachers, and administrators whose imagination and dedication has brought about both privatization and the other wide range of experiments that are attempting to improve schooling for all Americans.

1.

OUR BESIEGED PUBLIC SCHOOLS AND WHY THEY ARE PUBLIC

In many communities, public schools have become the schools of last resort for those who cannot afford the option of private schools, while those with means do whatever possible to avoid them.
                              Pedro A. Noguera, *Journal of Negro Education*[1]

Many Americans have lost faith in public schools. Stories of students carrying guns and schools unable to fix leaking ceilings and asbestos-lined walls reinforce the common view of public education as too overwhelmed by violence and bureaucracy to provide effective teaching. Whatever the more complicated truth about the vitality and problems of public schools, positive stories apparently hold little appeal. According to two U.S. Department of Education employees, when the department releases good news on student achievement, interest is scarce and reporting is "lackluster and negative, at best," but when the news is bad, the department is "jampacked" with media requests for additional information.[2]

Public schools have been blamed for our lagging industrial sector, our loss of national moral fiber, and the deterioration of our common values and religious beliefs. Public schools have been invidiously compared to Catholic schools and other private schools, which are said to be more orderly and to educate students better at lower costs.

Surveying Americans' views on public education is a notoriously difficult undertaking that often produces conflicting results. While a recent Phi Delta Kappan/Gallup education poll showed no drop in the popular rating of public schools over the past ten years,[3] a series of reports from Public Agenda suggested that such support is both extremely thin and increasingly endangered.[4] Just as important, Americans now face a concerted attack on public education by conservative groups who want to replace it with market solutions.

There have been recurring cycles of loss of faith in American public education: apocalyptic pronouncements about the failure of American schools go back thirty, fifty, even one hundred years. Nevertheless, the current cycle of disaffection has its own specific sources.

Since the early 1980s, business has been worried about our nation's loss of international competitiveness and has put pressure on public education to raise its standards. Although the warning in A Nation at Risk of a "rising tide of mediocrity"[5] was not explicit, criticisms about declining performance have largely been aimed at low-income students of color and at the urban schools that educate most of these students. The schools in these areas consistently suffer low levels of academic achievement; their graduates—and, even more, their large numbers of dropouts—are consigned to low-skilled, low-paying, dead-end jobs, prolonged careers in the underground economy, or early pregnancy, substance abuse, or incarceration.

Liberals and families of color have also become discouraged by the failure of public education to realize the promise of the Supreme Court's desegregation decision in Brown v. Board of Education. Among public officials and families of color, there is growing anger at the failure of public schooling to improve opportunities and outcomes for their children throughout the five decades since Brown. As Baltimore's Mayor Kurt Schmoke has pointed out, public school ". . . used to be a poor child's ticket out of the slums; now it is part of the system that traps people in the underclass."[6] This complaint has led Schmoke and others to experiment with privatizing public education, or has induced parents to create ways for their children to attend private schools.

At the same time, the protracted efforts that have been expended on behalf of equal educational opportunity, particularly through using student busing to desegregate schools, have created a backlash among some white families. In the 1960s, white parents in Virginia and other states created "free schools" for their own children as a way out of desegregation mandates. By now, such schools have formed their own long-standing constituencies; the parents, who are paying for private schools for their children in addition to supporting public education through their taxes, add angry fuel to the current privatization movement.

The persistent problems resulting from the nation's property-based method of school financing have become another arena of discontent. In both affluent and inadequately financed school districts, American families are aware that the growing gap between rich and poor families has exacerbated the disparity in resources available for public schools. Although "lack of proper financial support" ranked third in the list of educational problems mentioned by respondents in the Phi Delta Kappan/Gallup Poll, those surveyed also tended to believe that the existing U.S. system of funding for public schools is unfair to the average taxpayer.[7] Evidence of this uneasiness with how public schooling is supported can also be seen in the school finance battles that have generated protracted court cases in a number of states. These suits have attempted to equalize funding between property-rich, largely suburban school districts serving predominantly white students and poorly funded, often urban and rural, school districts serving low-income students, many of whom are children of color. Yet the equity cases have also exacerbated fears among middle-class and affluent families that the privileges of their status may be taken away, along with the competitive edge their children will need in a tightening economy. Insofar as school funding continues to be based on districtwide assessments of property taxes, middle-class families may well view their children's education as threatened by improving the terms of school financing for "other people's children."

Meanwhile, in our major cities, after substantial growth in the tax base during the 1980s, tax revenues have stagnated in the 1990s, at the same time as increasingly poor urban populations have generated greater pressure for public services such as mental health care, homeless shelters, and crime prevention. In many urban districts, the increasing competition for tax dollars has resulted in larger class sizes and teachers' salaries that lag behind those in suburban schools or in private-sector jobs.[8] Urban schools have also become old and run-down, and their facilities less equipped to prepare children for success in a high-tech society.[9]

The bifurcation of public education into two systems—one, commanding sufficient resources, for white, middle-class students and another, poorly funded, for children from low-income, generally minority backgrounds—has had its own vicious and self-perpetuating dynamic. Students who know that their schools do not have up-to-date books and the right equipment are less likely to work hard. Teachers who feel unappreciated or even under attack are less likely to perform with their full energy and creativity. Underfunded schools that show every evidence of becoming abandoned "orphans" also provoke increasingly hostile questions about the value of a public education.

To make matters more complicated, public schools, particularly in troubled cities, are being asked to respond to an increasing range of student needs generated by worsening economic conditions. Many middle-class and suburban families resent that public education has taken on the expanded responsibilities and costs of school meals programs, emergency and preventive medical care, counseling, violence prevention programs, and after-school recreation, as well as provisions for increasing numbers of students who do not speak English or who have disabilities.

Public education has also borne the brunt of an antiunion and antigovernment sentiment that has mushroomed around the country during the past two decades. In the eyes of many, government institutions, including schools, have allowed unions to protect workers who do little or nothing for their ample wage and benefits packages. Private companies, they believe, would cut the fat and show more spine in handling the wage demands of teachers or custodial staff.

The growing attack on public education has also been attributed to a long-term national decline in civic consciousness and public engagement, and an increasing privatization of all areas of life. Many activities that were once done collectively are now taking place in more isolated settings. Moreover, technology has replaced personal, face-to-face interaction in many spheres.[10] Insofar as our country's distrust of public institutions has increased, voter turnout has declined, as has working for political groups and parties. Political parties themselves have grown more tenuous. Among all social classes, there has also been a sharp drop in participation in civic organizations, from religious groups and labor unions to women's and fraternal clubs and neighborhood gatherings.[11]

This growing disregard for the importance of a common public sphere is self-perpetuating. People who participate in public schools and other political and social groups gain a sense of community and greater trust in civic life. Conversely, a decline in support for a varied and rewarding public sphere means that, with fewer avenues for joining with others in shared purpose, people turn inward and are more critical and suspicious of the commonweal. With little sense of the richness of public life, many see the benefits of a democracy narrowly: as the freedom to pursue their own private interests. The idea that any society must negotiate between individual and collective needs has become anathema to some and meaningless to many.

Finally, all these trends, particularly the growth of antiunion and antigovernment sentiment, have been fueled by the concerted efforts of conservative and religious groups. These groups have blamed public schools for the decline in Christian and other traditional values in our country, as well as branding them as part of "big government," and have crusaded to replace public education with free market solutions.

On the question of values, conservatives themselves have been split. Some, like former Secretary of Education William Bennett, have argued that public schools must teach students traditional American values, including honoring the flag and beginning the day with a Christian prayer. Other conservatives, however, believe the government's only role should be as "a guardian of individual liberty," and so have criticized both Presidents Reagan and Bush for valuing "freedom of the market place more than freedom of ideas," most pointedly for advocating prayer in the schools.[12]

To devise ways in which a free market ought to be injected into schooling, conservatives often take their inspiration from the libertarian Milton Friedman, who in the early 1960s proposed that American education be provided through vouchers. Friedman's voucher proposal was for a highly deregulated system, in which low-income families would receive no supplemental assistance and wealthy families would be free to use the vouchers to discount the costs of expensive private schools.[13] Conservatives have been joined by Catholic and other religious groups advocating for vouchers; they believe that public schooling has had a "monopoly" on education and want to secure public funding for private schools.[14] For some, the "separation of school and state is even more important than separation of church and state"; thus, all parents should be free to send their children to the school that espouses their particular beliefs and values.[15]

This mix of opposition to public schools has tugged at the once unequivocal support received by public education. The widespread sense of a public sphere under siege amid declining finances, poor performance, and conflicts over ultimate purpose and value has made school privatization seem an increasingly reasonable and plausible solution. According to their advocates, privatized schools will be businesslike, well-kept institutions. Freed from the rules and regulations that constrain the public sector, while boosted by competition and corporate know-how, such schools are bound for success, in the view of their supporters.

THE PRIVATE AND THE PUBLIC

Often prompted by declining tax revenues or government debt, privatization is an international phenomenon that takes place when a government sells assets, contracts out to a private company to deliver services, provides vouchers to individuals, or deregulates a public monopoly.[16] National, state, and local governments, as well as local government institutions such as school boards, have all used privatization to transfer responsibility for the delivery of educational services to private corporations.

The idea of privatizing functions of government is not new: under the assumption that there are specific efficiencies inherent in the private sector, governments at all levels have traditionally privatized many of their responsibilities. Some city governments, for example, privatize accounting, garbage collection, fire fighting, or parking meter maintenance—not always to their financial advantage.[17] Public schools have often privatized such areas as cafeteria services, transportation, and maintenance. Some schools have also contracted out to private companies to deliver special education programs to physically or mentally handicapped students; these contracted services have proved particularly controversial because of their extra expenses and because many feel that they segregate students unnecessarily.[18]

In 1995 the Minneapolis school board hired Public Strategies, Inc., a management consulting firm, to manage the district's schools; the president of Public Strategies now acts as the school's superintendent.[19] School districts in Baltimore, Dade County (Florida), Hartford, and elsewhere have contracted out the running and instruction of entire schools and districts to for-profit corporations. And the school board in Chelsea, Massachusetts, has contracted out to a nonprofit organization, Boston University, to run the entire district. (In both Dade County and Chelsea, the contractors raised their own money to pay or help pay for schooling.)[20] In Milwaukee, students from low-income families can receive educational vouchers from the city; the students may use these vouchers to attend any nonreligious private school willing to accept the modest sum as tuition.

Most privatization advocates want government bodies—usually the school board and the state—to be accountable for the effectiveness of the privatized schools. For example, the charter school movement, which is growing in popularity, has pioneered the drafting of legislation that allows school districts to contract out the running of a select number of schools to groups of teachers, museums or other nonprofit groups, and in some cases for-profit companies. But ultimate authority, as well as responsibility for the success of these ventures, is still maintained by the districts under charter school laws.

However, some conservatives want to eliminate altogether the government's role in monitoring and inspection. For these privatizers, government should be limited to raising the funding necessary for education. Even vouchers, which have been touted as a way to deregulate and ultimately abolish public schooling, are suspect to those who fear that, because public regulation follows public funding, vouchers may well become a way to smuggle public scrutiny into private schooling.

For the purposes of this monograph, privatization is defined as incorporating two major educational initiatives: 1) tax credits and/or educational vouchers given directly to families to be spent on either private or public schools; and 2) contracting out public schools or school systems to be run by for-profit companies. As will be shown, these two arenas of privatization have had at best mixed results.

Vouchers and tax credits, which allow families to choose their children's schools, have at times been presented as an expanded form of school choice. However, both vouchers and tax credits fundamentally redirect tax dollars as well as pupils. Under these schemes, although revenue for schools is raised through taxes, the educational funding stream flows directly from the government to private individuals without the mediation of a public system. Thus, education ceases to be a collective public undertaking and becomes instead a private relationship between each family and its school. Schooling ceases to be part of the public sphere; no longer a public service, it becomes a consumable item.

Those who include school choice in privatization argue that choice uses market mechanisms to drive school improvement. When choice is introduced, they point out, the "monopoly" that a neighborhood school has traditionally held over the residents in its catchment area is broken, and the school is forced to compete with other schools for its students. Thus, strong and effective schools will win out, and weak schools will be forced to change or close their doors.

While the argument for choice as a market mechanism is rhetorically compelling, there are several reasons for excluding the school choice movement from the rubric of privatization. First, most choice programs introduced into American education include only public schools. Second, in many public choice schools, decisions to improve curriculum or teaching or to close such schools continue to be made for a variety of reasons beyond simple competition for students. Third, in many districts, choice programs are combined with lotteries and other regulatory mechanisms to limit segregation by race, social class, or student ability. Thus, rather than being a form of privatization, school choice programs should more appropriately be viewed as one of the ways in which public school districts are creating careful regulatory policies to ensure quality and equity at the same time as expanding school offerings. Indeed, such choice programs offer an example of the vitality and responsiveness available within public education.

Contracting out to for-profit firms, of all the experiments on the current scene, has been the most controversial. Some educators have recently defended charter schools managed by private contractors as not being "steps in the direction of privatization," since the funds to sustain them are public and the schools remain accountable to public authority.[21] However, as the story of Education Alternatives, Inc., in Baltimore suggests, although the Baltimore public school system did retain the ultimate power over the company's contract, EAI was still attempting to serve two masters: the school district and its own stockholders.

More important than whether public funding should be used to contract out for private services is whether the providers are nonprofit institutions or for-profit corporations. When the providers of education are corporate, with clear financial objectives, their ownership stakes distinguish their company's schools from other schools along legal and political as well as economic dimensions. Consider, for example, these obvious accountability and equity issues: As a company seeks to maximize its profits, what mechanisms ensure that students receive a rich learning experience, including instruction in subjects that may not obviously advance test scores? What mechanisms ensure that those students who need extra time and attention to do well receive this more costly instruction? And, if school closings are a sign of health in a market system, how will those students who attend schools forced to close as a result of competition be protected from the disruption of their education?

The major privatization efforts thus far have targeted urban school systems that yield poor academic results and struggle under severe fiscal constraints. It is these school systems that, desperate for a way out, seek the relief that privatization promises. Yet privatizers have hardly been notable for the role that child development or pedagogy plays in their operating philosophies. Most privatization advocates are uninterested in questions of how children learn, or even what good classrooms look like. Not surprisingly, so far those privatizers that do offer descriptions of "break-the-mold"[22] classrooms have drawn their images from good public schools.

For many privatization advocates, schools are like any other business; privatizers assume that educational productivity, like the production of cars or hand cream, can be enhanced by market mechanisms. Yet this hard-nosed pragmatism about what works in the corporate world is based less on economic or political theory than on an intuitive, ideologically based certainty that "whatever government does, the private sector can do better."[23]

The idealization of business by recent privatizers in the United States has been accompanied by a devaluation of both the fundamental rationale for government initiatives and citizens' capacities for engaging in community activities and movements for reform. While stressing important ideals of individual liberty and freedom, privatizers deny the capacity of either voters or politicians to move beyond self-interest to embrace forms of civic participation. Leaning on social theories crudely derived from nineteenth-century Darwinism, they describe the market as more effective than government because it conforms to "our basic human instinct of operating in our own self interest."[24] Thus the awkward, often burden-some—and at times even unjust—steps by which democracy proceeds are described as failed alternatives that violate our very nature. Democratic participation, which involves individuals in a range of roles and responsi-bilities, is to be abandoned for narrow acts of consumerism.

Public education is more than a simple mechanism for delivering a commodity to consumers. Like other public institutions, it is a "vehicle for deliberation, debate and decision-making."[25] Through these processes, education becomes a public service that contributes to the comparative well-being and strength of both local communities and the nation as a whole. Insofar as education produces a more informed and responsible cit-izenry with a greater appreciation for the diversity of the cultures and tra-ditions of our populace, the entire society benefits.

Public education in the United States has been the key institution for assimilating successive waves of immigrants—a particularly important role today, as the nation experiences an enormous influx of people from coun-tries with different cultures and beliefs. Public schools have also been mandated to actualize the American promise that every citizen is "creat-ed equal"; that is, that success should be based on merit and not on hered-itary privilege. And public schools have been the locus for our continually shifting dialogues about civil society and the values and beliefs that bind us as a nation. The real danger of privatization, as Jeffrey Henig has point-ed out, is not that some students will be allowed "to attend privately run schools at public expense, but that they will erode the public forums in which decisions with social consequence can be democratically resolved."[26]

THE PLAN OF THE BOOK

By contrast with the rich understanding of public education's role out-lined above, the debate about privatization has largely been cast in market terms. While the larger roles and responsibilities of education are period-ically referred to in the course of this monograph, privatization is first evaluated largely on its own narrow terms. However, in the final two chap-ters, questions are raised about the purposes of education that would be jeopardized or lost by the withdrawal of education from the public sphere.

The next five chapters use five critical issues in education as lenses through which to view past and present experiments in privatization: stu-dent outcomes, costs, parental voice, accountability, and equity. Can pri-vatization or market-based solutions produce better student achievement for the same or lower per-pupil expenditures? What is the nature of

parental participation in privatized schools? Are market-based schools
more accountable to students and their families than traditional public
schools? Finally, can privatization deliver greater fairness than bureaucratic regulation in terms of racial desegregation and equalization of
resources? These five issues reflect the terrain on which the battle for privatization has been—and continues to be—fought. Before continuing, a
fuller description of each should be given.

EDUCATIONAL OUTCOMES. While student achievement in primary and
secondary public schools has not declined over time, a significant gap
exists between current student achievement and what young people will
need to know in the next century. Add to this concern the selling of privatization as the obvious route to improving student achievement, and
educational outcomes become a logical first criterion.

What has received less attention in the privatization debate is how
student achievement is to be measured. The only consensus reached at
the 1996 governors' and corporate leaders' education summit was that we
have no national standards for measurement and assessment. There is also
a growing concern among many educational reformers about the limitations of standardized tests. Yet newer approaches, such as portfolios of students' work, school quality reviews, and other, more authentic assessments
need perfecting before they can be accepted as substitutes. Privatizers,
however, working under pressure to secure quick, easily definable, and
inexpensive measures of success, have shown little interest in these
reforms.

COSTS. The cost of public schooling is of enormous concern to all
Americans. Not only do an increasing number of Americans without children in public school support education through their taxes, but the current, property-based method of taxation, which creates drastic inequities
in schooling between property-poor and property-rich districts, has spurred
protracted legal battles in more than two dozen states.[27]

Privatizers promise to make do with the existing system of funding in
strapped urban school systems; privatization experiments have generally
occurred in exactly these schools. Advocates take their inspiration from
Catholic schools, which have traditionally had lower costs than public
schools, in part because of lower administrative expenses, in part because
of narrower curriculum offerings, and in part because Catholic school
teachers are paid much lower salaries. Thus, one question is whether privatizers can achieve better results at lower cost without sacrificing the
increasing variety of vital services that public students now receive—particularly when there is also shareholders' expectation of drawing profits to

contend with. Beyond this, can privatization defuse the growing pressure for radical fiscal reform?

PARENTAL VOICE. Privatization advocates claim that the market will act as an adequate vehicle for the expression of parents' concerns about schooling. Parents want effective schools, and privatization theory holds that in a market-based system only effective schools will survive. But the opportunities children have in school are determined by more than choice. If parents are to influence what goes on, so that schooling works best for their children, they must involve themselves in a variety of general policies and specific school decisions.

In general, privatizers have focused on the narrow exercise of choice—parents can decide that their children will enter or leave a school. This form of influence is obviously most compatible with vouchers and similar systems. Instead of helping to improve schools through their participation, dissatisfied parents are simply to take their children elsewhere. However, other versions of privatization, such as contracting out schools, have occurred without using choice; there, parental voice appears even more limited than in traditional public school systems. Although privatizers only rarely mention the more participatory forms of parental influence, it is vital to evaluate the ways in which privatization has—or has not—enabled families to express those concerns relevant to their children's school experience.

ACCOUNTABILITY. One of the central arguments advanced by privatizers is that public schools are unaccountable; that is, they are not effectively answerable to anyone—parents or taxpayers in general. This is because they are hamstrung by bureaucratic regulation, which is the inevitable result of compromises among competing interests and thus part of the public-ness of public schools.[28] Unfettering schools from governmental control and subjecting them to the invisible hand of the market, privatizers argue, should make them both accountable and effective. The analysis here will focus on how and to what extent effective accountability has been, or might be, achieved under different forms of privatization. Since much of the bureaucratic accountability structure currently governing public education was introduced to guarantee access to students historically denied equality of opportunity, the analysis also focuses on whether freeing schools from regulation increases or undermines the rights of traditionally disenfranchised students.

EQUITY. In a public school system that offers universal access, academic achievement has remained highly correlated with socioeconomic status, race, and gender. Nevertheless, equal educational opportunity for all children has been a critical component in our national vision of schooling. The search for educational equity in the United States has concentrated on several areas: efforts to diminish racial isolation and the disparity in achievement between white students and students of color; policies to mitigate fiscal inequities arising from an uneven endowment of property wealth among districts; precautions to ensure that girls' special needs are not neglected; and measures to provide a fair and effective education to students with disabilities or whose first language is not English. As large-scale immigration continues, and the number of families trapped in deep and long-lasting poverty increases, these struggles for fairness are likely to grow fiercer and more critical.

Privatizers maintain that equity-related objectives will be better served through deregulation, and through provision of schooling by free enterprise rather than government. They promise not only to raise outcomes for poor students and students of color but to give these children the kind of educational choice and quality their more privileged peers now receive. This study analyzes the record of privatization efforts thus far and asks whether there are signs that, despite pledges to the contrary, school privatization may become a strategy to abandon our commitment to equity and replace it with a dual system of educational opportunity.

The next chapter reviews how advocates have argued for the benefits of privatization in each of these five areas. Chapter 3 describes two privatization experiments, one in performance contracting and one with vouchers, funded by the federal government in the 1970s. Chapter 4 analyzes the experience of Education Alternatives, Inc., in nine Baltimore public schools. Chapter 5 reviews four other contemporary privatization initiatives: the Chelsea-Boston University Partnership, the Chicago Corporate Community School, Hartford's EAI experience, and the Milwaukee Choice (voucher) Program. Chapter 6 describes current reforms in public education affecting the five areas. It suggests that public schools have not been monolithic, that a good deal of ferment is now occurring in the public education system, and that important functions are likely to be lost if public schools are exchanged for a privatized system. The final chapter summarizes the evidence on school privatization and concludes with observations regarding the importance of public education. It makes clear that, even if this privatization movement is halted, public education in this country will still face the challenge of creating a unitary, equitable, and effective public school system.

2.

THE PROMISES OF PRIVATIZATION

If one-quarter of the products made on an assembly line don't work when they reach the end of the line and another quarter fall off the line before the end, the solution is not to run the line faster or longer. Different production processes must be created. Put simply, the nation needs new ways to conduct the business of educating the young, and entrepreneurship must be at the top of any list of reforms.
Denis P. Doyle, Senior Fellow, The Hudson Institute[1]

The promises for how America's schools will be improved by privatization are motivated by a range of beliefs and imply quite different strategies. Some privatization advocates believe that free enterprise is the best way to run any institution. Others urge increased funding for Catholic, Christian fundamentalist, and other religious schools. Still others want relief for families wishing to avoid public schools because of radical libertarian or white separatist ideologies.

Some privatization boosters hope that the hundreds of billions of dollars spent on public schools annually will provide new investment opportunities. According to John McLaughlin, editor of the *Education Investor*, public education is a "new and promising growth industry."[2] Whether or not McLaughlin and other investors in education are right, there are twenty-five publicly traded companies in the education industry stock index, including educational management organizations like Education Alternatives, Inc., and suppliers of preschooling, special education, foreign language instruction, and services to at-risk youth. Education stocks—excluding textbook publishers and school supply companies—grew 65 percent in 1995.[3]

Predictions of how privatization will improve schools have shifted over the past fifteen years, partly in answer to criticisms by opponents and partly as a result of shifting stresses and new agendas within public education. Until the 1980s, concerns about equal educational opportunity for all students still dominated the national dialogue. Therefore, privatization supporters often promised that the market would naturally desegregate schools, as well as give low-income students the same freedom to choose schools that has always existed among upper-middle-class families. "Choice policies do the most for—and are most urgently sought by—the least fortunate members of society," asserted Chester Finn when he was deputy secretary of education under President Reagan.[4] Finn and others also saw privatization as eliminating bureaucracy to make schools more accountable to all parents, but particularly to low-income families, who would finally be able to choose where their children went to school.

In the late 1980s, equality and accountability became less central to privatization arguments. As the standards movement took a more prominent role in national public education discussions, privatization was increasingly advanced as a student achievement strategy. Despite the antiregulatory rhetoric that accompanied most such proposals, Finn and other leaders in the movement supported a strong governmental role in setting standards and establishing testing regimens.

Recently, in part because of severe school budget problems, particularly in large cities, the rationale for privatization has increasingly been framed in terms of the presumed efficiencies of the market. Privatized schools are claimed to be more streamlined, more effective, and less costly.

PRIVATIZATION AND STUDENT ACHIEVEMENT

Our schools are determined to liberate students as individuals; to develop in every child the confidence and capacity to think independently; to participate intelligently, work productively, and live happily in a free society.
Chris Whittle, founder of the Edison Project[5]

The most common argument for privatization has been that it will improve schooling through simple market mechanisms. When schools are forced to compete, good schools will draw students while poor schools will either improve or their classrooms will empty and they will be forced to close.

There are actually two sets of invisible hands that privatizers assume will create these beneficent market forces; those of parents and those of teachers and other school staff. While parents will choose the best schools for their children, as well as withdraw their children from ineffective schools, school staff will be prompted by direct and indirect incentives. That is, teachers will have to work harder to retain their students and their jobs, and their salaries can be based on performance.

Those privatization advocates seeking to extract profits from apparently lean urban budgets contend that further cost cutting will not harm students. "Will the desire for profit result in the neglect of students?" ask John O'Leary and Janet Beales of the Reason Foundation, a group promoting free enterprise. "Not likely. Businesses know that the surest path to prosperity is to please your customer."[6]

In contrast to these market-driven forces for improvement, the mass of regulations, requirements, and standards by which school boards and departments of education seek to ensure school quality are seen as cumbersome and ineffective. "The market is rational and government is dumb"[7] is a dramatic statement by a Republican congressional leader of this belief.

Yet, as critics of privatization have pointed out, the most common way of describing school outcomes—by students' scores on standardized tests—is primitive, yielding results that are incomplete and often misleading. Even when better kinds of information about schools are developed, producing and distributing such data, so that parents can make good choices, require considerable effort and expense. Equally important, families do not choose schools solely for educational reasons. The Carnegie Foundation's *School Choice* reports several surveys of families who were asked why they switched schools. In an Iowa district with an open enrollment plan, only 32 percent of those parents who wanted to leave their neighborhood school cited "educational benefits"; 36 percent cited "family convenience," 16 percent "proximity to job or home," and 10 percent "school philosophy or values." Similarly, a survey in Arizona found that only a third of the students who switched schools did so for academic reasons; the rest cited proximity to home, day-care, or work, specialized programs, sports or athletics, and other reasons.[8]

The assumption that, given the proper information, families will always choose the best education for their children is also contradicted by a study of African-American families in St. Louis. Confronted by a desegregation plan that allowed them to attend predominantly white schools with excellent offerings and high student achievement, many families chose to keep their children in poorly equipped, segregated schools with low levels of achievement, where they felt more comfortable.[9]

Though a number of studies make clear that families are happier with schools they have chosen than with zoned ones,[10] too many reasons other than academic ones enter into selecting a school for choice to be seen as a reliable force for ensuring educational quality. Equally important, despite parents' belief that schools they have chosen do a better job

than neighborhood or other zoned schools, evidence suggests that neither curriculum nor student performance is better under choice arrangements than in zoned schools.[11]

PRIVATIZATION, ACCOUNTABILITY, AND PARENTAL VOICE

*What schools need now is entrepreneurship, not change by rule, regulation,
and statute.*

Denis Doyle[12]

The attack on regulation and bureaucracy is a central tenet of privatizers.
Myron Lieberman, a longtime privatization advocate, believes that only
deregulation and private education can make schools more accountable.
In *Beyond Public Education*,[13] he argues that public schools have failed
because no one is in charge—not local governments, not the states, not
the federal government—and because each level of government is hope-
lessly hamstrung by regulations and bureaucracy. For Lieberman, the only
cure is to end public education and create entrepreneurial schools, which
will be accountable to their clients.

The premise that privatization will make schools more accountable to
students and their families begins with severe criticisms of current public
forums for parental voice and community opinion. Parent association meetings, school boards, state and federal regulations: all these forms for articu-
lating and executing public will on a variety of issues are judged both
cumbersome and ineffective. For Paul Hill, "American public schools have
become government institutions, not community enterprises dedicated to
the raising of children."[14] John Chubb and Terry Moe, whose *Politics,
Markets, and America's Schools* was a major influence in the privatization
debate, develop this point at great length. They argue that in a large, pluralist
democracy like ours, the "public will" is always a compromise among special
interest groups; as a result, all decisions must be carefully regulated and
monitored. In public education, this has resulted in a spiraling bureaucracy,
where no one is satisfied. Like other privatization advocates, Chubb and
Moe say that accountability must be shifted from a public effort to a private
act. Rather than having parents drag themselves to endless, unproductive
PTA and school board meetings, Chubb and Moe would have dissatisfied
families simply move their children to another school. Using the power of
consumers, these families would vote with their feet.

Politics, Markets, and America's Schools' policy leap from sketchy evidence has been critiqued elsewhere.[15] For Chubb and Moe, choice "has the
capacity *all by itself* to bring about the kind of transformation that, for

years, reforms have been seeking to engineer in a myriad of ways" (italics in the original).[16] This is because Chubb and Moe see the market as cus- tomer- or client-directed. As public schools are eliminated, schools will be released from their bureaucratic stranglehold, to "emerge in response to what parents and students want."[17] To avoid the controversial notion of vouchers, Chubb and Moe suggest that students, not schools, should receive public money—in the form of scholarships sent directly to those schools students choose to attend.

While choice is the panacea for Chubb and Moe, other privatizers believe that whole districts can be improved by being taken over by a single firm. In the latter case, the market force of parental choice is clearly absent. Nevertheless, the argument for privatizing school districts does take markets into account, reasoning that businesses can provide quality control through a "consistency of effort" that is unattainable in the public sector,[18] and that private companies offer accountability based on performance. As David Bennett of EAI stressed in 1993, the market mechanism was even more stark in Baltimore than under conditions of family choice: if the company's Tesseract program did not perform by raising students' test scores, the school board would simply end the company's contract.[19]

However, not all privatization advocates believe that the market alone—either through parental choice or performance contracts—can provide sufficient accountability. Beyond academic standards, there are also issues of ensuring equal educational opportunity. Thus, while Paul Hill argues that schools in this country should be contracted out, either to public or to private organizations, he maintains that school boards should be responsible for monitoring and evaluating the contractors' efficacy, and that state and national bodies should determine standards for preserving or enhancing equity as well as for scholastic achievement.[20]

PRIVATIZATION AND EQUALITY/DIVERSITY

We don't tell poor people what to eat; we give them food stamps. We don't tell them which doctor to go to; they have Medicaid cards. [Yet, in education, only the rich can] buy their way out, by moving into a certain neighborhood or choosing a private school.

Chester Finn, former
Deputy Secretary of Education[21]

Several different arguments have been made to support the contention that privatization will equalize educational opportunity for all students. The first focuses on race: the market is the best route to desegregating education because when there is choice *all* families will simply seek the best schools, regardless of whether their student composition is black or white.

This claim is boldly made by James R. Reinhard and Jackson F. Lee in *American Education: The Dynamics of Choice*.[22] In their view, vouchers are the obvious alternative to forced busing. Vouchers will enable inner-city students to leave their ghettos for the schools of their choice, thereby voluntarily desegregating education. (The authors do not expect white students to choose largely black schools.) Though Reinhard and Lee do not describe how strapped school districts can fund the elaborate, individually tailored transportation needs generated by such a system, they mention carpooling, special busing, and providing students with transportation money as ways of enabling students to travel wherever necessary to receive the best education alongside their more affluent peers.

The claim for privatization as a natural route to desegregation was advanced as a logical step after federal desegregation policy shifted away from mandatory interdistrict pupil transfers. A 1976 amendment to the Emergency School Aid Act (ESAA) authorized grants to support the planning and implementation of magnet schools in districts attempting to desegregate. The premise behind magnets was that, if schools in non-white neighborhoods were enriched with particular foci such as science or the arts, or hosted gifted programs, white parents would choose them for their children. Desegregation would become voluntary, and students would flow from black neighborhoods to formerly all-white schools and from white neighborhoods to previously black schools.

Magnet schools have had mixed success. Student achievement in magnets has generally been higher than in zoned schools, in part because students take more rigorous courses and in part because the students choose to be there, which also means that they are often students with more motivation than those who stay in the zoned schools.[23] Yet research about the effects of magnets on desegregation has been clear: when not bolstered by mandates that ensure mixing, magnets have not increased racial integration.[24] Moreover, because of the concentration of nonwhite students in inner cities, and the greater tendency of white urban students to attend private schools, minority students remain less likely to be with white students in public school magnets than they would be in private and religious schools.[25]

The second argument for how privatization benefits educational equity focuses more on the social class of the students. Proponents use two different approaches to make their case. One holds that privatizing the worst schools—those serving low-income, disadvantaged, generally inner-city students—is the radical surgery needed to make them more effective, responsive, and efficient. As John McLaughlin, editor of *The Education Investor*, argues, privatizers have targeted schools with "chronic" problems. "That's where the need is usually greatest, where the progress can be most dramatic—and that's where the money is."[26] Whatever the validity of the notion that profits can be extracted from financially strapped urban areas, this vision of privatization sees low-income students remaining in their own schools.

By contrast, Paul Hill's proposal for contract schools acknowledges current fiscal inequities. Hill assumes that, in order for contracting to work, schools and districts around the country must all have the same per-pupil amounts to spend. "By bringing all schools up to true equality of funding, contracting can dramatically, and promptly, increase funding for schools in the most troubled inner-city areas."[27]

Another approach to equity focuses on vouchers and other forms of privatization that involve allocating school finances directly to families. It assumes that low-income students will use their vouchers to leave the run-down and poorly equipped schools they currently attend and enroll in the better schools of their more affluent peers. The problem of assuming that families choose schools only or largely for educational reasons has already been discussed.

Vouchers also raise a number of questions concerning implementation in the context of families' widely differing capacities to pay for schooling out of their own pockets. Will all children be given vouchers for the same amount? Will families who can afford to add to the voucher and pay for a more expensive school be allowed to do so? How will middle-class families, who have always enjoyed superior schooling, be convinced to relinquish this privilege in order to give all American children an equal chance?

Although many voucher advocates leave these questions unanswered, Myron Lieberman suggests in *Privatization and Educational Choice* that vouchers be means-tested, "providing low-income parents with higher vouchers than middle- or high-income parents."[28] Clearly, ending or reducing the disparity between students in low-income and affluent school districts, as Hill urges, would also go a long way toward solving the educational problems of inner-city and rural students. Yet Hill's and Lieberman's proposals tend to make light of decades of middle- and high-income school districts' struggles, through costly legal and legislative battles, to maintain their financial edge over neighboring, low-income districts. The question of how to reorganize school financing to create genuine equality of opportunity among all students remains unsolved by privatizers.

There is a third and quite different line of thinking about the advantages privatization offers "the least fortunate members of society."[29] This argument focuses on diversity. Its proponents maintain that because a market system is customer oriented, vouchers and other forms of privatization can target their offerings to students with different beliefs, values, and academic needs. As Lieberman has put it, rather than having to "satisfy everyone or even a majority of parents," for-profit schools need only establish their "marketing niche."[30] Chubb and Moe make a similar argument: in a public education system "the majority, or, more frequently, the most powerful minority, determines what will be done," and even those who do not like the decision have to go along with it.[31] By contrast, privatization will make possible smaller schools geared toward the interests and demands of varied constituencies. Chris Whittle, the media entrepreneur and creator of The Edison Project, a line of for-profit schools, wants his schools to be thought of as "an educational version of Home Depot, McDonalds or Wal-Mart."[32]

The power of the market to tailor products to customers with diverse needs has also been taken up by supporters of Catholic and other religious schools. In *Choice in Schooling: A Case for Tuition Vouchers*, David Kirkpatrick contends that Christian fundamentalists, Catholics, and others with specific beliefs have been forced into either accepting a free education at the cost of their personal values or preserving their values at the cost of the financial assistance others receive. This state of affairs is the result of our false notion of education as a builder of a common American culture. In Kirkpatrick's view, the United States does not need such a common culture, or if it does, perhaps television rather than schools should be the one to build it. Although he concedes that choice in schooling will lead to sharper differences of opinion among citizens, which may well contribute to increased divisiveness, he regards this as nothing to fear. "Hitler and Stalin knew that pluralism of democracy is inherently divisive. However, they did not realize how unified we can become to defend our *right* to differ."[33] Like the great dictators, he says, the foes of privatization favor social conformity over democracy and pluralism. Indeed, he accuses them of being afraid of "those who think or act differently from themselves."[34]

Though images of democracy as a diversified marketplace appear to respond to our country's new immigrant populations as well as to its increasing economic stratification, the implication is that bringing students together to create a common culture has proved too difficult. The vision these privatizers offer is of a splintered nation in which families choose schools that match their different incomes, values, and educational philosophies while schools, like discount suppliers, find their market niche. Unfortunately, these depictions obscure severe racial and class cleavages in our society and too glibly transform privilege and disadvantage into matters of personal belief and cultural taste.

PRIVATIZATION AND SCHOOL EFFICIENCY AND COSTS

You can't make a light bulb out of a candle. And interestingly, a light bulb is now cheaper than a candle. The Edison Project is of a similar mind about education. We want to start over.

Chris Whittle[35]

The promise of greater efficiency and lowered costs has been an increasingly dominant theme in the movement for privatization in recent years, as school districts have come under growing financial stress. The problem of balancing declining budgets has been an important source of districts' interest in privatization. The commonly accepted belief is that private companies are "lean and mean." They can do anything that government can at a much lower cost. Competition keeps quality up and reduces price. An early book on privatization articulated the promise in its title, *Better Government at Half the Price! Private Production of Public Services*. Its authors declared, "As every taxpayer knows, government is wasteful and inefficient; it always has been and always will be."[36]

If government is too timid or weak to trim inefficiency and waste, business offers three clear solutions: cutting back on personnel, particularly those whose performance does not meet high standards; lowering wages; and eliminating benefits. Chris Yelich, president of the American Association of Educators in Private Practice, boosts his cause with the assertion that "contracting can help schools offer a wider variety of classes while holding down overhead." He is referring to health insurance, pensions, and the significantly higher wages paid by public schools than by private schools. The premise is that private companies will show more spine than government in resisting worker and union demands. Janet Beales of the Reason Foundation, which promotes free enterprise, makes this claim explicit. "Since the cost of labor is often lower in the private sector, overall efficiency is enhanced by using the private sector, particularly for labor-intensive organizations, such as education."[37] Beales cites Department of Education reports showing that base salaries for private school teachers are 37 percent lower than in the public sector, and she points out that, should student enrollment drop, privatized schools can quickly lay off teachers. However, even if salaries are lower and security nonexistent, Beales believes that privatization still offers teachers something: being a "private practitioner" who sells a specific service brings freedom and a professionalism not available to public employees.

The attack on unions is also an increasingly explicit aspect of the privatizers' critiques of public schools. "Monopoly of schools is not the only obstacle to achieving workable competition and the efficient allocation of resources," write Simon Hakim, Paul Seidenstat, and Gary Bowman. "Teachers' unions are resource monopolies that have strong influence over the price of labor and the production of the school."[38]

The charter school movement, which currently straddles public and private education, incorporates individuals with a range of motivations, including one strand that is strongly antiunion. While new charter school legislation in some states allows only individuals and nonprofit groups to organize charter schools, other legislation allows for-profit organizations to set up their own schools. Charter school advocates often argue that their schools need neither collective bargaining nor—because accountability for school quality will be determined by student outcomes—teacher certification. If untrained individuals working for low wages and without benefits can raise student achievement, this is presumably all that counts. Yet lowering teachers' salaries makes a profession that is struggling to compete with others to attract qualified individuals even less competitive.

Until now, the arguments for the capacity of privatization to solve the problems afflicting public schools remain relatively untested. Similarly, the hazards and costs of this experiment are still largely unexplored. Nevertheless, clues exist from trial runs over the past two and a half decades. They suggest cause for some optimism, but for more concern, in each of the five areas selected for evaluation: student outcomes, costs and resource allocation, parental voice, accountability, and equity. Using these five areas, the following chapters explore to what extent the promises made for privatization have been realized in schools and school districts across the country.

3.

Two Forgotten Experiments in School Privatization:
Performance Contracting and Educational Vouchers

If an extra $20 billion a year would bring slum children up to the academic level of their suburban rivals, some legislators would support the expenditure out of idealism. But many legislators feel—and not without reason—that even if they gave the schools an unlimited budget, the children of the slums would continue to grow up both personally and academically crippled.
Christopher Jencks, *The Public Interest*[1]

The early 1970s evoke images of a very different time: anti-Vietnam War protests come to mind, as does public awareness of poverty and prejudice brought about by a strong civil rights movement. While President Johnson had been undone by his promise of "both guns and butter," there was widespread faith in the ability of the government to solve domestic problems. Though Nixon occupied the White House, a stream of federal initiatives continued to emanate from the Office of Education and the Office of Economic Opportunity.

The Nixon years ushered in a surge of faith in the ability of free enterprise to improve public education, particularly for disadvantaged students. During the early 1970s two critical educational experiments—performance contracting and educational vouchers—were initiated by the Nixon administration. In both, the federal government injected forms of market mechanisms and privatization into public education. Contracting out the teaching of basic skills to businesses was expected to bring private ingenuity and accountability to bear on the achievement of disadvantaged students. Similarly, vouchers were to give more control over schooling to poor and minority parents at the same time as they spurred public schools to experiment and innovate. Although the two experiments went about it in very different ways, both were devised as strategies for gaining tighter control over public education systems that had grown too large, too expensive, and insufficiently responsive to the needs of students.

The stories of these experiments are rich with the peculiarities of the early and mid-1970s. Nevertheless, they offer complicated lessons for those interested in today's privatization movement. What is odd is not that solutions similar to those being proposed now have already been tried, but that so little serious attention has been paid to the lessons of these earlier experiments.

PERFORMANCE CONTRACTING

The idea of performance contracting as it emerged in the late 1960s had several predecessors, both inside and outside education. In the 1920s and 1930s, for instance, the tenure of many rural teachers working in one-room schools was dependent on the scores of their eighth graders in required statewide tests given in each subject. If all or most of the students passed, the teachers were reemployed; if not, the teachers were let go.

Performance contracting emerged in the Department of Defense during the Vietnam War as a way of gaining greater control of skyrocketing military production and costs. The idea also had its champions in the Office of Education, which sought greater accountability in the variety of programs it was funding through Head Start, the Elementary and Secondary Education Act of 1965 (ESEA), and other initiatives. "Contracts and federal funds, whenever possible, should be performance contracts," Associate Commissioner of Education Leon Lessinger wrote in a 1969 issue of the *Phi Delta Kappan*.[2] Lessinger, an engineer, had come to education from the Aerospace Foundation, and he was shocked to find his new field without paradigms of accountability for productivity and quality. Since performance contracting demanded that companies sign "a contractual agreement to perform a service . . . according to agreed upon terms, within an established period, and with a stipulated use of resources and performance standards,"[3] Lessinger believed it would ensure accountability in public education.[4]

THE TEXARKANA STORY[5]

Through the influence of Lessinger and others in Washington, performance contracting in education got its first chance in a small town on the Arkansas/Texas border. Texarkana's population of 60,000 was about 75 percent white and 25 percent black in 1969. With the aid of Model Cities money, Texarkana was renovating housing in its black neighborhoods as well as merging several previously all-black and all-white schools. As in many school districts, administrators in Texarkana saw the low test scores of black students as a major obstacle to integration. The common view was that these students needed some form of rapid remediation before being placed alongside their white peers. ESEA was authorizing money for dropout prevention, and the Texarkana school district secured funds from the U.S. Office of Education for the 1969–70 school year.

Dorsett Educational Systems, Inc., a small firm producing audiovisual equipment in Norman, Oklahoma, was hired to instruct approximately 350 students, both black and white, identified as being two years or more behind grade level. Dorsett's contract called for the students to gain one grade level in both reading and math after eighty hours of instruction, for which the company would earn a base payment. If the students gained more than a grade level, or reached grade level in less than eighty hours, the company would earn extra payment. In addition, Texarkana promised to buy Dorsett's learning technology at the end of the performance contract. This was to be the "turnkey" phase of the project; once the effectiveness of the private-sector initiative had been demonstrated, the public schools were to adopt its methods as part of the regular school curriculum.

The Dorsett Rapid Learning Centers were carpeted and air-conditioned trailers parked adjacent to the schools. Each was staffed with one teacher and one paraprofessional. The targeted students left their regular classes for two hours every day to attend the Rapid Learning Centers. Most students were assigned to one hour of reading and one hour of mathematics. Instead of textbooks and other conventional curricular materials, they sat in front of teaching machines that used filmstrips synchronized with sound. Students answered questions by pushing buttons on the machines; when a question was correctly answered the filmstrip moved to the next frame. Because the students proceeded at their own rate, the program was said to offer individualized instruction.

In the late 1960s and early 1970s, the low test scores of African-American students were often attributed to poor motivation. This simplistic and condescending explanation dovetailed nicely with the programmed instruction offered by Dorsett and other performance contractors: not only was learning to proceed by responses to stimuli, but concrete, tangible rewards were offered to increase the students' motivation. Dorsett offered Green Stamps and radios for completed lessons, and a television set was promised to the outstanding student at the end of the year.

With desegregation on the national agenda, the 1969–70 academic year put the town of Texarkana on the map. Dorsett's Rapid Learning

Centers received eight hundred visitors and seven hundred requests for information. To meet the swell of public interest, a principal who was also acting as project director traveled across the country, making speeches and attending conferences on Texarkana's performance contract program.

Dorsett's contract with the district had cut out tasks written into the ESEA proposal for funding, including developing study habits and improving speech and grooming. Moreover, Dorsett was not offering instruction in science and social studies, as it had initially promised the district. Since the company's fees were tied to students' test gains in math and English, these two subjects became the focus of all Dorsett's efforts. At the end of the year, while the Rapid Learning students tested above those of a control group in some areas, their scores proved to be invalid because they were found to have been exposed to most of the test questions. The discouragement of students who had worked all year to improve their performance can be inferred from the failure of many to pick up their radios; the prize television lay unclaimed. "Teachers Teach to the Test," the local newspapers proclaimed. As Don Rader, a teacher then in his first year, recently recalled, "I had come in as an idealistic teacher. It was discussed at Sunday School. There were all those headlines. I thought, Gosh, you just don't teach to a test!"[6]

At the same time, an obvious concern for the school district was how or whether Dorsett should be paid. The firm claimed—correctly—that there had been no guidelines for admissible practice regarding the similarities between the questions asked on exercises and on tests, and that it had merely been trying to ensure the best possible student achievement. Not surprisingly, there was widespread recognition that testing ethics needed to be firmed up. The Educational Testing Service was called in to provide guidelines for subsequent contracts.

In 1970–71, with funds from the Office of Economic Opportunity, Texarkana continued its experiment in performance contracting with a larger company, Educational Developmental Laboratories, Inc. (EDL), a division of McGraw-Hill. Although this second contract included a bonus based on students' performance, EDL received a substantial fixed charge, half of which was to be paid up front. EDL used Dorsett's trailers, with only slight changes. Like Dorsett's, EDL's programmed instruction relied on reading machines and other hardware. However, EDL did not offer any external motivators. At the end of the second year, student tests—designed this time by the Educational Testing Service—again yielded disappointing results. EDL had guaranteed one year's gain for all students, but only 41 percent had made such a gain in reading comprehension and just 31 percent in mathematics.

Nevertheless, Texarkana proceeded with a third year of performance contracting, once more with EDL. This time, EDL teachers were under less pressure to cover a set program, and they supplemented EDL's curriculum with a variety of other materials. Thus, the third year was less a demonstration of a specific instructional program than of the value of privatizing learning. Among the third year's objectives were a decrease in the dropout rate, a jump in attendance, and of course a rise in achievement—though this time the goal was only to get 75 percent of the students to make one grade-level gain. At the end of the year, the dropout rate among participants had increased from 5.4 percent to 6.8 percent; attendance had declined and was slightly worse than the overall average attendance in the targeted schools; and while only 38 percent of the students in the EDL program made one grade-level gain in reading comprehension, the record was still worse—28 percent—in mathematics.

THE SPREAD OF PERFORMANCE CONTRACTING

Enthusiasm for performance contracting quickly spread far beyond the Texas-Arkansas border. A 1970 national survey showed two out of three school board members in favor of the practice.[7] Whereas only two performance contracts had been let out by school districts in 1969–70, there were sixty during the 1970–71 school year, worth a total in excess of ten million dollars.[8] Eighteen of these new contracts were supported by the Office of Economic Opportunity. In addition, more than forty contracts were sponsored by states and individual districts, often using money from various federal programs. For example, the Colorado Department of Education funded innovative reading programs in certain school districts using performance contracting. Michigan, Virginia, and California were involved in similar state-supported projects. Numerous urban school districts, including Gary, Indiana; Flint, Michigan; Portland, Oregon; and Philadelphia initiated their own contracts. The numbers continued to rise. By the 1971–72 school year, more than 150 performance contracts, most of which were based on technology-driven instruction, were let by public school districts around the country.[9]

The major national teachers' organizations reacted with concern for their financial security, faced with the prospect that salaries were to be based on student performance or that they might have to compete with private firms. However, performance contracting was rapidly accepted by other powerful groups. As one contemporary observer put it,

In mid 1971, performance contracting appears to be popular with the current administration in Washington because it encourages private business to participate in a traditionally public responsibility. It is popular among some school administrators because it affords new access to

federal funds, because it is a way to get new talent working on old problems, and because the administrator can easily blame the outside agen-
cy and the government if the contract instruction is unsuccessful.[10]

A survey of superintendents conducted in April 1971 confirmed these
reasons for their enthusiasm for performance contracting and added another: the widespread belief "that performance contracts would offer greater
returns for dollars spent."[11]

THE OEO STUDY OF PERFORMANCE CONTRACTING

Government activism in education during the Johnson-Nixon years
was accompanied by several large-scale field studies of the federal interventions. In 1968, the Department of Health, Education and Welfare
instituted planned variations in both its Head Start and Follow Through
programs in order to compare several alternative approaches to providing educational and social services for disadvantaged children. With various federal agencies funding performance contracting in Texarkana and
elsewhere, there was strong sentiment in Washington that the government should evaluate the merit of this new strategy.

In 1970–71, the Office of Economic Opportunity initiated a one-
year national experiment to ascertain whether private educational firms
could teach disadvantaged students to read and write better and more
cheaply than local public schools. Eighteen large and small school districts were chosen to participate in the OEO study. The districts included
such cities and towns as Dallas; Chicago; Gary; Gilroy, California; Wichita;
Jacksonville; Grand Rapids; Cherry Creek, Colorado; and of course
Texarkana.

Within each of these districts, the schools chosen to participate in the
experiment had to demonstrate serious academic problems as well as meet
the criteria for federal assistance under Title I. Within each school, those students judged to be most behind academically were selected for the experiment, and a near equivalent group was selected as controls. While the
experimental and control students were generally from low-income backgrounds, the schools differed in their ethnic composition, with some schools
being largely black, some Mexican-American, Native American, or white.

To carry out the performance contracts in the eighteen districts, the
OEO selected six private companies, which would be rewarded on the
basis of how much progress students made during the academic year. In
addition to having had some experience with educational materials or
instruction, the companies had existed for at least a couple of years and
were said to be responsible and stable. However, like Dorsett, most were

small firms trying to break into the education field. Thus, the OEO performance contracts offered them the chance to demonstrate their learning systems and educational technology to a national audience and so obtain follow-up contracts as well as gain new markets.

While all the companies featured individualized instruction through some form of programmed learning, they varied in the degree to which their methods were technology based. Teaching machines, audiovisual equipment, and filmstrips were featured. In addition, some companies offered material incentives to students and some did not. Finally, companies varied in the extent to which they controlled the classroom schedule and details of instruction or relied on the creativity of teachers. All were free to alter the educational program they offered during the year as they saw fit.

As both proponents and critics of privatization would lament, the experiment mixed the influence of several not easily isolable factors on student learning: a variety of instructional methods and educational technologies; the use of material incentives; and private management working under performance contracts. This mix made it difficult to attribute causality to the results. Some of the projects also experienced start-up problems, so that students did not have the benefit of a full year of instruction. And some schools suffered significant attrition among the experimental students, making it necessary to substitute children from a secondary experimental pool. Moreover, the complications of pre- and post-testing of experimental and control students in multiple schools in twenty different cities made any assessment of costs difficult.

Nevertheless, enthusiasm for the project ran high, and observers in and out of government expected the results of performance contracting to be positive. Thus, shock prevailed across the nation when Batelle Laboratories, which had been hired to conduct the testing, released its cautiously tabulated test results. Put simply, the nationwide differences between gains by the experimental and control students in reading and mathematics were minimal. While the experimental pupils did slightly better in reading, the control youngsters did slightly better in mathematics. When the performance of students in the experimental and control groups was compared in subjects not taught by the contractors—spelling, language, science, or social studies, for instance—students in the control group generally did better. Most important, the achievements of the experimental students fell far short of the promises of the private companies, to say nothing of the changes necessary to eliminate their deficiencies.[12]

These findings aroused a torrent of critiques and arguments. As some critics pointed out, the experimental and control groups were not strictly comparable. Moreover, even under the best conditions (which had not occurred), testing technology was still relatively unsophisticated, and performance contracting seemed "a haven for the misinterpretation of scores."[13] Others pointed to flukes that could have influenced the results, including speculation that teachers in the control classes might have tried harder during the year because they felt threatened by performance contracting.[14] Nor have attacks on the OEO experiment stopped as the years have gone by. In 1989, Myron Lieberman invoked the project, calling its failure the fault not of performance contracting but of the students, who were "largely intractable to remedial treatment."[15]

By 1974, with controversy continuing unabated, two additional federal reports were produced to analyze the OEO project: the Department of Health, Education and Welfare funded one by the RAND Corporation and Congress asked the Government Accounting Office (GAO) to conduct another.[16] While the GAO report criticized several aspects of the OEO experiment's design, both reports generally agreed that the performance benefits and cost savings from privatizing instruction were negligible at best.

Can anything be said about the various teaching strategies of the companies? A reanalysis by the Brookings Institution in 1975 tried to address this question. The study found that two companies, Learning Foundations and Singer/Graflex, had poorer attendance than did their control schools, although their test scores were not lower. Only one company, Quality Educational Development Corporation, making moderate use of machines and incentives to students and employing paraprofessionals for half of all staff needs, improved students' test scores by an amount that could be considered significant. Another, Westinghouse Learning Corporation, similar in its handling of technology and incentives but with paraprofessionals representing 80 percent of staff, did worse than its control schools. As the Brookings study concluded, a heavy reliance on machines and paraprofessionals did not seem the best strategy.

Convinced that payments to the companies could not be withheld based on low test scores, the Office of Economic Opportunity offered rather generous settlements. But some of the participating companies refused to reach agreement. Two companies told GAO investigators in late 1972 that they had "sustained high financial losses and injury to their reputations as a result of their participation."[17] And a 1975 study reported that, of the six firms, "one went bankrupt, two more dropped direct classroom work, and all six stopped accepting incentive-based contracts." Three years after the close of the experiment, half the firms still had not settled with the OEO.[18]

BANNECKER ELEMENTARY SCHOOL[19]

With all the controversy surrounding the OEO study, it is fortuitous that several other case studies of performance contracting are extant. One of the most important and best documented is of an elementary school in Gary, Indiana. The value of the Bannecker Elementary School experience lies in its comprehensiveness, giving it a consistency unattainable by the OEO experiment. Performance contracting at Bannecker was set up to run for three years. The company chosen, Behavioral Research Laboratories (BRL), was given responsibility for running the entire school, including every aspect of staffing and instruction. Unlike other performance contracts, this one did not select students: Bannecker under BRL was composed of the same students as before. The hope in Gary was similar to that which had fuelled experiments in Texarkana and elsewhere, and continues to fuel today's experiments: that with an incentive-based contract a private firm would undoubtedly raise student performance. Moreover, the firm could be fired if it failed.

In 1970, when the school district contracted with Behavioral Research Laboratories to run the Bannecker School, Gary was a steel mill town of 182,000, with half of its labor force working for U.S. Steel. Gary also stood at the forefront of urban problems: it had a decaying business district, air pollution, growing crime, a shriveling tax base, a high degree of residential segregation, and racial tension. Three-fourths of Gary's public school population of 47,000 students attended inner-city schools, and approximately 60 percent of the total were African-American.

Nearly all of Bannecker's 850 students and most of its teachers were African-American, as was its principal. Although the school was located amidst well-cared-for, single-family homes, Bannecker served an inner-city neighborhood. Of Gary's thirty-three public elementary schools, Bannecker ranked thirty-first on reading and math scores.

In 1970, Behavioral Research Laboratories was ten years old. The company had made its reputation and profits from programmed reading and math materials. Originally created for the military by the linguist William Sullivan, the materials followed a behaviorist, stimulus-response model of learning. Because they were printed on newsprint, they were cheap to reproduce and easy to give away—as rewards, students were allowed to take home completed lessons. Title I compensatory education grants, which helped schools offer enrichment materials and other remedial instruction, had provided BRL with the chance to enter the public school market. Its pitch was its willingness to work with "students that nobody else wants."[20] The company quickly created some successes in Dade County, Florida, and the Ocean Hill-Brownsville district in Brooklyn. Several public schools in Gary were also using the Sullivan materials when, in spring 1970, BRL approached the district superintendent with the idea of taking over an entire school. In addition to its

contract with Bannecker, the firm secured two other performance contracts that year: in Philadelphia and in Monroe, Michigan.

Given freedom to rearrange the school, BRL attempted to create
joint leadership with Bannecker's principal. A junior high-style organization was adopted; students were scheduled to move from room to room for
different subjects. Grade levels were eliminated, and students were grouped
according to ability, but they were to be advanced as soon as their knowledge in a certain subject area increased. Even special education students
were integrated into regular classes, a measure that was seen as innovative
by some and cost cutting by others.

Viewed pedagogically, the Sullivan approach was "materials oriented";
viewed from a budgetary standpoint, BRL substituted instructional materials and paraprofessionals for professional teachers. While the school curriculum included language arts, mathematics, social studies, science, arts
and crafts, music, drama, and physical education, most of BRL's resources
focused on reading and mathematics. An observer entering the school
after BRL was in operation two months saw only the two subjects being
taught.[21] This was both because BRL did not manufacture materials in
other areas and because its performance contract was based on reading
and mathematics. If *any* student did not achieve at the national norm in
reading and mathematics at the end of the three years, BRL was to refund
all the fees paid by the city of Gary.

The first year of the experiment at Bannecker was beset by problems
for both the school and BRL. In October, the Gary teachers' union threatened to strike over the lack of licensed teachers and the large class sizes at
the school. In January 1971, the Indiana General Education Commission
removed Bannecker's accreditation. The decommissioning report cited lack
of state-adopted textbooks, insufficient time apportioned in subject areas
like social studies and science, conflicts between the duties of the principal
and those of BRL's representative, the use of six unlicensed teachers, and
higher than permissible pupil-teacher ratios. The report also noted that,
despite BRL's emphasis on reading, library records suggested students were
doing less reading on their own initiative. By March, however, after
changes were made in staffing and some new curriculum was added, BRL's
legal problems were rectified and the school was reaccredited. A first-year
RAND evaluation called the instruction in areas other than reading and
mathematics "relatively conventional."[22]

How did all this experimentation and controversy influence
Bannecker students? While attendance was the same or higher than in
previous years during the first half of the term, during the third quarter it
dropped below Bannecker's and Gary's average, and it slipped still further
in the fourth quarter. If some attributed the lower attendance to the greater

freedom allowed by the BRL program, others blamed it on the lowered morale caused by the strife roiling the school.

Achievement in reading and mathematics was similarly trouble-some for both Bannecker and BRL. By the end of the 1970–71 year, although progress differed at different grade levels, slightly better than 40 percent of all students had made a year's gain in reading, and two-thirds had made a year's gain in math. Put differently, while the proportion of Bannecker students who were at or above national norms had advanced from one-fourth to about one-third, this was a far cry from BRL's goal, and the company was on its way to having to give a substantial refund to the city.

Equally interesting, the pressure to maximize profits had gone beyond BRL's advertised instructional method to influence more subtle aspects of teaching. An analysis of Bannecker's first-year test scores suggests that teachers ignored students at the extreme ends of the achievement con-tinuum and concentrated on those in the middle range. Compared with a national sample of students, middle-range Bannecker students improved more, while high- or low-performing students improved less.[23] The Gary contract rewarded BRL only for students who achieved normal district levels in reading and mathematics at the end of each year. Since the best students could reach the goal on their own and the worst might not reach the desired level even with a lot of attention, the company's practices were responding to the incentive structure written into the contract.

Several major changes occurred at Bannecker during the 1971–72 school year. First, enrollment dropped from 800 to 700 students. The conflicts between BRL and the principal over leadership were resolved by hiring a new principal. The school also returned to a more tradition-al elementary school setup, so students no longer moved from class to class. Although the reduction in enrollment would have allowed BRL to reduce Bannecker's teaching staff, conflicts between the union and the contractor led to all the teachers being retained—and consequently to a lower student/teacher ratio than in the previous year.

Although instruction continued to rely heavily on the Sullivan materials in reading and math, during the summer a number of Bannecker teachers had worked to formulate activities and learning objectives in language arts. These resources were being pilot tested in Bannecker at the same time as they were already being marketed nationally by BRL. To resolve apparent conflicts over BRL's profiting from techniques developed in part at Bannecker, the Gary school district was to receive 2 percent of the royalties from the sale of all materials. As to whether other schools in Gary might also use these teach-ing aids or other aspects of Bannecker's program, a RAND evaluator pro-vided a poignant no: "In Gary the cleavage between the black and white communities has led the white schools to regard programs developed in black schools as inappropriate to their educational needs. Consequently, . . . it is hard to see that there will be any widespread turnkeying."[24]

In the spring of 1972, the Gary schoolteachers staged a 22-day strike, leaving Bannecker with less than the 150-day school year provided for in its contract with BRL. As a result, BRL canceled its year-end testing developed for evaluation and payment. According to observers, half or fewer of the Bannecker students were expected to reach the performance level the company needed to qualify for payments.[25]

The contract between Gary and Behavioral Research Laboratories was canceled prematurely, in the fall of 1972. And in 1978, after accusations that the company had given kickbacks to a public official in order to secure a multimillion-dollar sale of reading materials to the Ocean Hill-Brownsville district in Brooklyn, BRL went bankrupt.

SOME LESSONS FROM PERFORMANCE CONTRACTING

Despite the differences between current realities and the 1970s, there are some obvious conclusions to be drawn regarding performance contracting. First, whatever the difficulties of testing, neither the Texarkana, OEO, nor Gary experiments resulted in significant student advancement even in narrowly defined areas of reading and mathematics. Moreover, the three experiences in contracting raise questions concerning instructional methods, staffing, governance, parental voice, testing, and costs, in addition to the general debate over the wisdom of turning schools over to private companies. All these issues are currently being discussed as schools and school districts contract out more of their instruction to private firms.

INSTRUCTIONAL METHODS. Although the educational companies involved in performance contracting described themselves as providing individualized instruction, what they meant was that their curricula could be followed by an individual student at his or her own pace. The companies also described their instruction as materials-based, signifying that, while the instructional methods sometimes gave teachers more opportunity to work with a single student, personal contact with teachers decreased as students were directed more by the self-guided instructional program built into the technology and curriculum materials.

Race may not have been considered in choosing instructional methods that routinized students' lessons and minimized their contact with teachers. Yet, as a contemporary proponent of privatization made clear, the prevailing view was that the problems of disadvantaged students were "relatively clear-cut" and largely motivational. Thus, the competitive world of business became a natural source for learning systems that included "a range of extrinsic and intrinsic rewards."[26] Indeed, most of the performance contracting companies relied on crude notions of motivation to stimulate learning in students who might well have had complicated reactions to finally being legally allowed to attend desegregated schools. But the materials- and technology-based curriculum could not have reassured African-American students trying to adjust to nervous and often hostile white students and teachers. With the advantages of hindsight, it is striking that the instructional methods chosen further isolated already marginalized students, rather than enhancing personal contact and trust among students and teachers.

Finally, company-run classrooms tended toward greater uniformity than comparable classrooms in the school system at large. This was in part because the curriculum stressed materials-based instruction and in part because the pressure on the companies to raise achievement caused a certain inflexibility in their approaches to education:[27] the capacity of contract teachers to adapt to the variety of specific needs of different classrooms actually decreased, even though the companies claimed to offer "individualized instruction."

It is impossible to isolate the different effects of programmed instruction, decreased student contact with teachers, and the heavy use of learning machines and other technology. Fashions in learning-theory change; behaviorism and programmed instruction are now largely out of favor. However, as subsequent chapters will explore, current for-profit companies are no less interested than were the companies involved in the OEO experiment in converting relatively expensive professional staff into less expensive materials and equipment.

STAFFING. Most of the companies offering performance contracting in the early 1970s hired certified teachers, primarily because teachers' unions in school districts across the country insisted. However, in addition to relying on technology and paraprofessionals to keep costs down, companies relied on one particular means of stretching resources: class size was generally larger in the OEO sites, as well as at Bannecker, than in comparable Title I Compensatory Education classrooms.

GOVERNANCE. Performance contracting was introduced to circumvent educational bureaucracies and eliminate the red tape so evident in many schools. Accountability would be clear-cut: success or failure at coaxing student gains in achievement. Yet performance contracting seemed to make life more complicated in many ways. Teachers complained that contracting increased their routine clerical work, as they responded to requests for regular reports on students' progress. The need for coordination between school administrators and officials in the companies also caused problems, and it required an increase in the number of individuals in administrative roles.

Many districts that engaged in performance contracting during the early 1970s contracted out for both instruction and management support, often to two different companies; thus, a second group of outsiders was frequently introduced. Because company performance needed to be measured by an independent evaluator, yet another group of outside professionals took part. If payments to companies based on test score improvements made accountability appear a simple matter, the truth was more complex in daily school life. Not surprisingly, in a survey of superintendents conducted in 1970–71, management complications were considered one of the strongest disadvantages of performance contracting.[28]

PARENTAL VOICE. Although the late 1960s and early 1970s witnessed a variety of efforts to empower low-income communities, performance contracting was never meant to increase parents' voice in schooling. Indeed, families remained noticeably outside these experiments; accountability was framed to serve company and school district requirements.

TESTING. The experiments in performance contracting exposed the weaknesses of the tests available in the early 1970s. Although payment to the companies was to be based on student improvement, standardized tests were shown to be insensitive to the gains made through a specific curriculum and unreliable measures of an individual student's progress. However, as the experience in Texarkana with Dorsett showed, the use of special tests that might be painstakingly tailored to a particular curriculum created an environment conducive to teaching to the test. If there was any common agreement about the results of performance contracting, it was that testing needed improvement.

But performance contracting also significantly narrowed educational concerns in the experimental districts, as student achievement, even in reading and math, was defined in terms of measurable test gains. Indeed, even without the specific instances of teaching to the test, performance contracting became the first prominent example of what would become a growing national concern: the power of testing to reshape curriculum and teaching according to the dictates of improving test results instead of broader student learning.

COSTS. Despite predictions, performance contracting did not noticeably reduce educational costs, even when compared with labor-intensive school programs like Title I. Although based on their results the educational firms in the OEO project were entitled to earn an average of only 33 percent of their potential fees, OEO subsequently made a number of adjustments that substantially increased payments. Even before these adjustments, OEO had awarded $6,883,220 in contracts to reach a total of 12,000 students, for an average cost of $573.60 per student. All these numbers seem low by today's standards. However, by calculating reading and math as two-fifths of a teacher's work, one program evaluation estimated that the OEO performance contracts cost at least twice as much as traditional instruction. It concluded, "There may be some merit to the position of some; namely, that if the schools had the same amount of money to improve reading and mathematics programs as used in the OEO experiment, they could do a better job of teaching."[29]

USING THE PRIVATE SECTOR TO DELIVER INSTRUCTION

What may strike the observer most about performance contracting is how much cutting-edge educational technology has changed in the past twenty years. In the 1970s, the best the market could bring to schooling were teaching machines and audiovisual devices. Now we live in a world of computers, which week by week offer increasingly sophisticated learning programs. Indeed, companies like EAI and Edison promise to bring the latest in these developments into the schools. Yet despite today's more complex devices, the performance contracting experience has much to say. Whenever learning is technology based, two issues must be addressed. First, to what extent can technology be effectively substituted for student-teacher contact? Second, can learning be made teacher-proof—as most providers of computer-based courses of study claim?

While current companies contracting to school districts are not basing their fees on how well they can raise students' performance and testing has grown much more sophisticated in the past two decades, their contracts *are* being renewed on the basis of test scores. Moreover, as the stock price fluctuations of Education Alternatives, Inc., suggest, when a company is traded on the open market, its profits rise when public confidence responds to evidence of increasing student achievement. Such high stakes are likely to focus learning very strictly on instruction that can create newsworthy increases in test scores. But such high stakes also work against richness and experimentation.

Clearly, the companies that took on performance contracting in the early 1970s were change agents—as are the companies offering their instructional programs to schools and school districts today. Yet another, more questionable, parallel exists: the targeted students—the guinea pigs for both performance contracting and current privatization experiments—

are poor and of color. A quarter-century ago and today, frustration with educational failure and a respect for corporate effectiveness has led to districts asking business to intercede. Yet contracts with commercial firms create another layer of distance between schools and their students. If, as past and present proponents of vouchers claim, the real spur to school improvement is accountability to clients, then the experience of performance contracting suggests that the market may remove local schools from the control of families and students, even as it makes them responsive to distant stockholders.

VOUCHERS AND THE ALUM ROCK EXPERIMENT

The story of vouchers takes place during the same heady and exploratory period as performance contracting. A successful voucher program depends on parents, teachers, principals, and district administrators all making decisions that shape schools—and so the experiment, by its very nature, was subject to compromises as it developed in the community.

The idea of educational vouchers goes back to the early 1960s, when the conservative economist Milton Friedman argued that vouchers would improve educational efficiency by placing schools in a laissez faire market. Friedman's idea was to give parents of American children vouchers equivalent to the money being spent by their public schools to take to whichever schools, public or private, they wished to attend—the public/private distinction would soon evaporate. If a family had the money and wanted to supplement their voucher in order to afford a more expensive school, they were free to do so.

In the late 1960s, the voucher idea reentered American policy circles through Christopher Jencks and other radical critics of education. Theirs was a totally revised concept: Jencks wanted poor families to receive more money than the middle class in order to equalize the educational opportunities of all children. For him, not only did vast differences in expenditures differentiate public schools for middle-class children from those for poor children, but, particularly in large cities, public schools were mired in defensiveness and timidity. Jencks also believed that public schools were not necessarily more responsive to poor children, and private schools were not necessarily more elitist. The latter had indeed catered largely to middle-class and wealthy students but would likely be more receptive to low-income students if they were given the same amount of money as the more privileged to spend on their education.[30] Jencks's enthusiasm for vouchers attracted others who hoped that they would help save the faltering public school system by supporting free schools and other alternative schools that were emerging in low-income neighborhoods.

In 1969, the Office of Economic Opportunity launched an experiment, in which Jencks and his associates played a major conceptual role. The OEO voucher experiment sought to temper what would be an educational free market with regulations to protect equality and avoid discrimination. For example, lotteries of potential enrollees would be combined with student choice to ensure that no school became predominantly poor or minority. The OEO assumed that disadvantaged families, who had been poorly served by public schools, would have a natural interest in floating such an experiment. Leaders in several state and local governments initially appeared interested in trying a voucher program, particularly since federal money was involved. But, as OEO representatives moved across the country they found that many groups representing poor and unorganized constituencies were afraid that vouchers would help whites escape desegregation and choose all-white schools. Resistance was also strong not only in the teachers' unions but among school boards and school bureaucracies. If parental choice had a comfortable, populist ring, many educators saw competition for students as having some nasty implications: most obviously, pressure from students to attend popular schools might well mean that others would close, costing jobs held by teachers and principals.

By 1971, after two years of trying to stir up interest in vouchers, only a single district was willing to sign on for five to seven years of a voucher experiment. Alum Rock, California, was a small, dusty, and financially strapped school district serving 15,000 largely black and Chicano low-income students.[31] The superintendent hoped to use decentralization to create more flexibility for innovation; if OEO produced money for decentralization, he would accept a modification of OEO's regulated compensatory voucher plan. Two changes, further moving the experiment away from any model of laissez-faire capitalism, were key to Alum Rock's agreement. First, by California law, the experiment could begin with only public schools. Even when the legislature finally enabled nonpublic schools to enter the demonstration in fall 1973, Alum Rock as a poor area had no private schools available. Second, teachers who no longer had sufficient students to form a class because of the voucher experiment would be reassigned elsewhere—no one would lose a job as a result of consumer preferences.

The voucher demonstration began in six schools, each containing minischools. With funding from Washington for decentralization, teachers were free to revise their curriculum, create more flexible student groupings, and in other ways reorganize the school day. Not surprisingly, many teachers reported never having worked so hard. After the first year, a number said they were burned out.

An OEO-paid office, the Sequoia Institute, handed out information on schools as well as vouchers. Although the Institute was formed to represent parent interests, it was in effect a new layer in the bureaucracy—and a thorn in the side of many Alum Rock educators.

The conflict between the Sequoia Institute and the rest of the district was most obvious in issues that set schools competing against each other. Though teachers and principals liked the idea of creating schools with different foci and strengths, they were reluctant to countenance marketing these differences to attract pupils. Principals resisted advertising and other comparisons that would encourage parents to believe that one school was better than another. The district's commitment to increase the power of principals through decentralization conflicted with OEO's goal of encouraging parent power through choice, via the Sequoia Institute. Since teachers were not rewarded for higher enrollments by raised salaries, they were not anxious to attract new students to their schools. The discrepancy between market values and what might be called professional values has been put this way by David K. Cohen and Eleanor Farrar: "Teachers wanted better working conditions: room to breathe, to prepare, to teach, perhaps even to invent. Voucher advocates wanted better market conditions: to improve educational performance by turning up the competitive heat."[32] After the first year, Alum Rock teachers and administrators put further controls on the market by insisting that each school be given enrollment limits. The overflow from popular schools was now sent to less appealing sites.

Nor were low-income parents natural "consumers" of education. In contrast to OEO's assumption that parents would be pleased by the expansion in educational options for their children, their first concern was to obtain squatters' rights for their children to attend their own neighborhood schools. Although eventually some parents did choose nonneighborhood schools—about 10 percent in the second year and 18 percent after that— their number remained modest. In the course of the demonstration parents learned more about their children's schools, yet their knowledge remained shallow. Most knew what they knew from official communications, and most were pleased with their children's schools as they stood.

From a complicated experiment that spanned five years a couple of conclusions can be drawn. While vouchers contributed to increasing the diversity of instructional programs in Alum Rock, innovation was encouraged more by decentralization and increased teacher autonomy than by competition among schools. An experiment intended to boost the power of parents perversely resulted in the opposite, as teachers and principals emerged from the demonstration with greater control—while parents had little more say than beforehand. An evaluation done in the late 1970s summarizes these outcomes:

> The assumption underlying the original scheme was that schools were bad because parents were powerless, and that parents were powerless because they had been excluded by professionals anxious to protect themselves from popular control. If parents had more power—which in this case was to be gained by control of school funding—it was expected that professionals would then be accountable and that schools would thereby be better places for children. But when some barriers to parent involvement were removed, power distributions did not change appreciably.[33]

Do the revised plans and surprising findings in the voucher experiment mean that Alum Rock has little to tell us about schools and the market? On the contrary. One important lesson that Alum Rock offers is that neither school personnel nor parents and students act in ways predicted by free market theory. Most important, when it comes to schools, parents given the opportunity do not for the most part seize the initiative to expand choice. This reluctance among low-income families to choose has since been replicated in a number of other experiments over the past twenty years. However, few parents of any social class appear willing to acquire the information necessary to make active and informed educational choices.

Second, although market theory holds that teachers and other school personnel will vie to expand enrollment, this is not what actually happened. True, the terms of the Alum Rock experiment put a lid on entrepreneurial activities by professionals. Yet, beyond a certain class size, no increase in teacher salaries can compensate for carrying more students; teaching more children to read is difficult and labor-intensive. Similarly, why should principals help put their colleagues out of business when some fluke of enrollment may put their own school out of business the next year? Even now, twenty years later, when many school districts have succumbed to the pressure to publish test scores, strong professional ethics prevent rivalries that elevate one school at the expense of another.

CONCLUSION

The lessons of the privatization experiments of the 1970s are worth remembering as our country embarks once again on experiments with vouchers, contracting out schools to private companies, and other forms of privatization. For some, the experiences with performance contracting and vouchers showed only how difficult it is to conduct experiments in education. Yet there is a related conclusion, less often drawn: for the same reason that simple trials of education reform are nearly impossible, simple remedies are also an illusion.

Beyond the question of improvements in student achievement, the encounters with vouchers and performance contracting also show how two very different approaches to educational accountability unfold. If vouchers had the unexpected result of increasing the power of public school professionals rather than parents, performance contracting clearly removed control over schooling from teachers, school administrators, and parents. Parents in particular virtually disappear from school policymaking under performance contracting. Thus, assertions that a program will make schools more accountable must also ask questions about who really benefits from such accountability.

4.

PRIVATIZATION IN BALTIMORE, 1992–95

In a sentence, we either dramatically improve student performance with-out spending more money or our contract is canceled. That's what I call accountability!
     John Golle, chairman and CEO, Education Alternatives., Inc.[1]

Baltimore, a former steel town, faces many of the challenges typical of American cities—a declining economic base, constrained public sector revenues, and widespread poverty. The 183 schools in the Baltimore City Public Schools system (BCPS) serve 130,000 students, of whom 82 percent receive a free or reduced-price lunch. According to a recent Government Accounting Office report, the average Baltimore student "is a poor, African American child living in a female-headed, single-parent house-hold."[2] Even with large numbers of students involved in compensatory education programs, BCPS's test scores have ranked among the lowest in the state, and the dropout rate has hovered around 14 percent, compared to a statewide average of 5 percent.[3]

Despite comparatively low administrative outlays, the Baltimore City Public Schools have ranked at the bottom of Maryland's twenty-four school districts in spending for regular instruction. In 1991, a study of inequalities in the Maryland system found that to bring the Baltimore City Public Schools up to the average per-pupil expenditures in the state would require an additional $26,250 per classroom.[4]

Education innovation is not new in Baltimore. In the late 1980s, with strong backing from its mayor, Kurt L. Schmoke, Baltimore began a variety of innovative educational experiments.[5] The public school system was the site for Robert Slavin's Success for All program, the first attempt to use Chapter 1 funds schoolwide to improve learning in the early grades.[6] When Maryland initiated a statewide Challenge Schools program for schools with low attendance and performance, twelve of the twenty-seven designated targets were Baltimore middle schools.[7] Two other programs, TIPS (Teachers Involve Parents in Schoolwork) and the Family-School Partnership, backed by Baltimore's Fund for Educational Excellence, were investigating new ways to improve teaching effectiveness and parent-teacher relations. Several public schools were also experimenting with BERRI, a computer-driven curriculum. With support from the Abell Foundation,[8] the BCPS was developing a reputation as a "laboratory for incorporating a number of private-sector resources and public/private collaboratives into its operations."[9]

In 1991, Dr. Walter G. Amprey became the new district superintendent. Given Baltimore's financial problems, as well as its inclination toward experimentation, it seemed a logical development when, in June 1992, the Baltimore City Public Schools hired Education Alternatives, Inc. (EAI), a for-profit corporation based in Minneapolis, to run nine of its schools: one primary school (prekindergarten through second grade), seven elementary schools (prekindergarten through fifth grade), and a middle school (sixth-eighth grade).

THE INTRODUCTION OF EDUCATION ALTERNATIVES, INC.

Both supporters and opponents of privatization in Baltimore would agree that the experience was controversial. Moreover, controversy appears to have characterized the efforts of Education Alternatives, Inc., long before its Baltimore enterprise. In 1986, in the course of its transformation from a subsidiary of Control Data Corporation to an independent corporation, questions were raised about its designation as a minority-owned firm.[10] EAI's initial contracts were in Eagan, Minnesota, and Paradise Valley, Arizona, where its early successes were used as a basis for its public stock offering in 1991.[11] However, in 1993, analysts raised questions about EAI's reported revenues and stock sales by executives.[12]

In fall 1991, Education Alternatives raised more than $2 million to showcase its instructional approach, "The Tesseract Way," in a third venture at South Pointe Elementary School in the Miami-Dade County public school district.[13] An enthusiastic review from South Pointe described EAI's Tesseract method as involving the latest in educational thinking. The teacher had become "a coach, facilitator, model, guide, and mediator," who was granted unprecedented professional autonomy in exchange for being charged with accountability for student performance. Students were reportedly becoming "self-regulated" learners, who puzzled over problems alone or worked in cooperative groups. Through authentic (non-multiple-choice) testing and tasks built on "real life experiences," critical thinking was being developed. And parents were allowed to help develop the educational goals for their children during quarterly parent-teacher conferences.[14]

To expand the company's capacity for involvement in public education, in December 1991 Education Alternatives, Inc., formed an alliance of four firms known as the Educational Alliance. While EAI itself was responsible for running the instructional program according to the Tesseract model, Johnson Controls, the largest janitorial service in the United States, was to provide maintenance; KPMG Peat Marwick, an accounting colossus, was to initiate computerized accounting; and the Computer Curriculum Company (CCC) would offer SuccessMaker, an instructional technology system.[15]

Baltimore City Public Schools' contract gave EAI approximately $27 million a year, calculated according to average per-pupil expenditures in the district, including Chapter 1 and special education funds. The contract was to run for five years, beginning with the 1992–93 school year.[16] Although many support personnel would work directly for EAI, the Baltimore public schools had a strong American Federation of Teachers (AFT) local of 8,500 members; thus, the contract stipulated that administrative and teaching personnel would remain employees of the Baltimore City Public Schools, with provisions negotiated by the union left intact.[17] This was to be EAI's first major venture. Using Tesseract and computerized instructional programs and its expanded capacity to improve operational efficiency, the firm promised immediate and dramatic improvements in student achievement in its nine schools.[18]

Although publicized as a performance contract, Baltimore's deal with EAI did not set forth performance standards for the four companies in the alliance. As Norman J. Walsh, then an associate superintendent in Baltimore, has since written, "Unfortunately, none of the procedures that the school system and the city have historically taken to safeguard the public interest when awarding contracts for public services was given the slightest heed." Calling the contract process with EAI "extremely odd," Judson Porter, the school district's finance officer at the time, remarked, "You don't put out a bid, you don't negotiate the best price you can possibly get, and quite frankly, [Amprey has] operated as an advocate of the company since."[19]

Difficulties were encountered during the early stages of implementation in the fall of 1992. EAI began by training teachers in the new programs and by making improvements in physical facilities at the nine schools, including floor and locker repairs, repainting, and furniture and plumbing restoration. But the SuccessMaker instructional technology was not ready until several months after the start of the school year.[20]

Early in the contract period, conflicts arose with the Baltimore Teachers Union (BTU), beginning with a dispute over EAI's replacement of seasoned, neighborhood paraprofessionals, who had been earning $10,000–$20,000 annually, with recent college graduates, who, as interns, were paid $6,000–9,000 annually and suffered extremely high turnover rates.[21] Compromise was reached by allowing those paraprofessionals who had college degrees to remain.[22] EAI also transferred all counselors and specialists, including teachers of art, music, physical education, and special education, out of the Tesseract schools, eliminating nearly one hundred instructional positions in the eight primary/elementary schools.[23] In addition, the company cut costs by offering teachers less than their standard training rates for attending Tesseract training and by cutting teacher planning time. Salaries for custodians in EAI schools were cut from an average of $11.00 per hour to $8.75.[24]

EAI's cost cutting in special education and compensatory education programs was no less controversial. In any urban district, a good deal of the money spent on education comes from state and federal money for low-income, low-achieving students who need extra help (Chapter 1, Compensatory Education, now called Title I) or for students who have been diagnosed as having particular disabilities (Special Education). While compensatory education has traditionally been carried out in "pull-out programs," special education has been accomplished through a range of programming, but particularly through special classes. Over the past several years, an "inclusion" movement has resulted in Title I money being available for schoolwide improvement in poverty-stricken areas, as well as in efforts to bring special education students into regular classes whenever possible. However, both policy shifts have been accompanied by clear rules that guarantee a continuing, high level of programming and services. In EAI schools, by contrast, both compensatory education and special education students were simply brought into regular classes, and the omission of specialized personnel and small-group instruction were supposed to be made up for by spending more time on computers.[25]

A first-year analysis of EAI's budget by the BCPS Department of Research and Evaluation showed that while EAI spent 62.5 percent of its Baltimore budget on regular instruction, the BCPS spent 72.3 percent. EAI also spent 5.6 percent of its budget on special education, compared to 11.2 percent by the BCPS. Conversely, during its first year EAI lavished more than double the amount provided by the BCPS for facilities (18.5

percent vs. 9.2 percent) and three times the amount for security (1.4 percent vs. 0.5 percent).[26]

The "Early Implementation" report by the Baltimore City Public
Schools' Department of Research and Evaluation, issued in January 1994,
was very measured. The report complimented the company for the "dramatic improvements in school facilities." It also described the implementation difficulties EAI had experienced during the first year, including
delays in the installation of the Computer Curriculum Corporation's
SuccessMaker and problems with hiring the interns. Interviews conducted by the BCPS with teachers in the Tesseract schools showed 11 percent
very satisfied, 42 percent fairly satisfied, 28 percent somewhat satisfied,
and 18 percent not satisfied.[27] The report, however, criticized increased
demands on teachers, insufficient training in the Tesseract method, and
poor use and high turnover of interns.[28]

"The Private Management of Public Schools: An Analysis of the EAI
Experience in Baltimore," released by the American Federation of Teachers
in May 1994, took a more aggressive stance than the district's report. The
AFT document, which covered the first year and a half of the EAI contract,
cited more absenteeism and declines in student test scores in EAI elementary schools, whereas attendance and performance in non-EAI schools had
shown modest gains. It also raised questions about financial accounting, special education, cuts in teaching staff, increased class size, and instability in
classrooms. In addition, the AFT noted that although instructional spending in EAI schools was lower than in other BCPS schools, EAI had initially
received as much as $500 per student more.[29]

Although there were plans to expand EAI's role in Baltimore, continuing controversy prevented this.[30] Moreover, the conflict with the
union continued into 1993–94,[31] when the BTU filed suit against the
school district, charging that the delegation of school management to private enterprises violated the city charter and denied local citizens their
right to decide how public schools should be run.[32] Threats of layoffs, calls
for the superintendent's resignation, and low teacher morale all appeared
to be by-products of the privatization initiative.[33]

Special education was a particularly troubling area in the EAI schools,
in part because Baltimore's special education program had been under
scrutiny since the 1980s. Baltimore was already engaged in a decade-old
legal battle resulting from its failure to comply with federal law on the
length of time handicapped students had to wait for formal evaluations and
services such as physical therapy and psychological counseling.[34]

EAI's waiver from the state of Maryland allowed it to move a majority
of elementary students with special needs from self-contained classrooms
to regular classrooms under three conditions: that the children's parents

approved; that the Individual Education Plan required by law for all children in special education was incorporated in the personalized education plan that EAI students were supposed to receive; and that a formal review of the new placements would be held within ninety days.[35]

The AFT, which had been monitoring EAI's special education program, asked the U.S. Department of Education to investigate whether EAI had violated federal law. The Department of Education in turn requested that the Maryland Education Department investigate.[36] Among the state's findings were that, of the 396 special education students that EAI had placed in regular classes, only in 16 cases had parents given their consent; that teachers in the EAI schools had not participated sufficiently in student placement decisions, and many remained unaware of students' disabilities; and that the mainstream classes failed to meet the disabled students' requirements.

According to the state's report, violations at the Tesseract middle school exceeded the total number of violations at *all* other Baltimore public schools. The Maryland Department of Education directed the city to craft a plan to correct violations by August 1.[37] The U.S. Department of Education meanwhile charged the state of Maryland with "poor supervision of special-education programs in EAI schools," and a federal judge ruled that in the future a court-appointed team would have to monitor key staffing decisions in the BCPS.[38]

As a result of the investigation, Maryland awarded special education students at the Tesseract middle school with 136,893 compensatory hours of education.[39] EAI's plan was to enable the three hundred students to make up 120 hours in a summer session run by three teachers, three interns, and three college students. The AFT called this a "questionable practice,"[40] and a contempt hearing was brought by the BTU. In the agreement eventually reached, the Baltimore City Public Schools admitted that the system was in substantial noncompliance with the Maryland consent decree.[41]

The controversial nature of the privatization initiative carried on into its third year, 1994–95. The city school system admitted that achievement gains reported in the previous spring were overstated, prompting charges by city council members and countercharges by EAI.[42] Superintendent Amprey's closeness to EAI was also called into question,[43] and the mayor warned that EAI's fate in Baltimore would depend both on improving student achievement and on the results of an independent evaluation, commissioned by the BCPS, being conducted by the University of Maryland. The effects were felt well beyond Baltimore, as the price of EAI stock dropped sharply.[44]

Criticisms of EAI by the union, and of the union by EAI, continued.[45] With an upcoming reelection campaign in mind, Mayor Schmoke

proposed a renegotiated contract with EAI, this time with explicit performance criteria.[46] By April 1995, the Baltimore city council's EAI
Financial Oversight Committee, created after a lengthy hearing the previous December, had compiled a five-page list of unanswered questions
concerning Education Alternatives' financial activities. Although the
committee identified few new concerns, it showed the major issues left
unclassified in the BCPS-EAI contract: problems with contract implementation, failure to provide budget and financial information about Title
I spending, attorney costs, special education, subcontractor finances, and
EAI's corporate financial activities.[47] By August 1995 some resolution
appeared to be in sight. But the situation changed when, on September 1,
the University of Maryland-Baltimore County issued an independent
three-year evaluation report showing only modest improvement in
achievement in EAI schools.[48] Once again, whatever understanding EAI
had with the district was in jeopardy.

THE UNIVERSITY OF MARYLAND EVALUATION REPORT

Given the heated atmosphere that surrounded the privatization initiative in
Baltimore, an unbiased evaluation report took on particular importance.[49]
Since any educational initiative like the EAI contract in Baltimore is complex and multidimensional, any sophisticated evaluation of the effects is
likely to be subject to diverse interpretations. Moreover, the UMBC evaluation was not a classic scientific experiment, or even an experimental evaluation of a social program: the real world impinged on the research in ways
that complicated the interpretation of the results. For example, the Tesseract
schools were evaluated by comparison with an equal number of control
schools; however, after EAI exerted pressure, several of the specific control
schools were changed by the Baltimore City Public School evaluation unit
in 1994. The Department of Research and Evaluation substituted for the
original control group three schools whose students had been somewhat
lower-achieving in the year prior to implementation of the contract with
EAI than students in the EAI schools.[50] This is a complication with
unknown effects. The UMBC evaluation report notes, "Changing comparison schools once they were named was irregular. . . . It is important to point
out that, in contrast to the statement, 'EAI was handed the worst schools in
Baltimore City,' the schools designated as Tesseract schools, while including
many schools that were among the most challenging schools in Baltimore
City, represented a mix of student achievement levels."[51]

    This section of the report uses the five criteria set out earlier—edu-
cational outcomes; cost; parental voice; accountability; and equity—to

review and interpret the University of Maryland-Baltimore County (UMBC) report. Before turning to the specific findings in these areas, however, it is worth presenting the general assessment from the evaluation report:

> The accomplishments of Educational [sic] Alternatives, Inc. in the management of seven elementary schools in Baltimore City are considerable, particularly in the area of change in classroom instructional practices toward varied activities, flexible grouping and a focus on the individual student. The initial test score decline [from 1991–92 to the first year of the contract, 1992–93] was substantial, with the lost ground recovered only by the end of the third year, and early implementation problems were accentuated by the opposition of the Baltimore Teachers Union. However, EAI would not be faulted for the level of change already accomplished in Tesseract schools were it not for the public's expectation of immediate and substantial change, and the symbolism of a "really different education" implied by the Tesseract name. Nevertheless, the early problems have been largely resolved and the infrastructure for program management is now in place. Change takes time and there has been an investment in the first three years that can be recouped by continuation. Should the Tesseract program continue through the last two years of the contract, EAI has an obligation to effect real improvement in the schools that they have been managing and to demonstrate an excellent urban education program. In turn, it is important that Baltimore City have an appropriate monitoring mechanism of the EAI contract and its components.[52]

One other fact is important to state at the outset: the per-pupil costs in the Tesseract schools were 11.2 percent higher than in the comparison schools.[53] Thus, this was not a case of equal spending.

OUTCOMES

The UMBC evaluation report noted that too much instructional time was being devoted to testing, and particularly to test preparation, in all Baltimore City schools. However, the preoccupation with test scores, and the concomitant use of instructional time for examination and preparation, was particularly evident at Tesseract schools, where, instead of moving toward less testing, EAI had added a fall test.[54] As for test scores, the UMBC evaluation report used several tests to compare the Tesseract schools over several years against the control schools. In general, during the three years of the initiative, the Tesseract schools first declined, then improved, so that they ended the period studied in a similar position to the comparison schools, with neither group making significant gains. As stated in the evaluation report for student scores,

> Over three years, scores for Tesseract students decreased and then increased to about the pre-program level. 1994–95 total reading NCE [National Curve Equivalent] scores on the Comprehensive Test of Basic Skills (CTBS) decreased one point from the pre-implementation year (1991–92) scores for the Tesseract schools but were unchanged for comparison schools. Total reading scores increased one point for Baltimore City schools, and total mathematics scores increased two points.[55]

A similar finding was reported for overall school scores:

> For Tesseract schools, changes in reading scores from 1991–92 to 1994–95 ranged from a six-point gain to a seven-point loss, and changes in mathematics scores ranged from a seven point gain to a five point loss. Reading scores increased in three schools, decreased in three schools and were unchanged in one school. Mathematics scores increased in four schools and decreased in three schools. Comparison schools had a similar level of loss and gain, and a similar number of losing and gaining schools. The Tesseract program has been effective in raising test scores in some schools but not in others.[56]

The evaluation report presented detailed reading and mathematics scores from the Maryland School Performance Assessment System, and the results were similar to the CTBS testing. Clearly, if privatization was expected to produce large differences, the results were disappointing.

Two other categories were examined: attendance and special education enrollment. In terms of attendance, there were similarly modest improvements in the Tesseract schools, the comparison schools, and the Baltimore City schools altogether.[57] The area of special education enrollment showed a large difference between the Tesseract and comparison schools. In 1991–92, the preimplementation year, 8 percent of enrollment in what would become the Tesseract schools, the comparison schools, and in all the schools throughout Baltimore were eligible for Level IV special education services. While this percentage dropped to 7.5 percent in the comparison schools and 5.6 percent in all Baltimore City schools in 1994–95, it fell precipitously to 2.7 percent in the Tesseract schools. When students who are eligible for special education Levels II, III, and IV are combined, the changes from 1991–92 to 1994–95 were

15.4 to 14.2 percent in the comparison schools, 15.0 to 12.0 percent in all Baltimore City schools, and 15.1 to 7.9 percent in the Tesseract schools.[58]

Although these changes are dramatic, the UMBC evaluation report did not investigate whether the services that these pupils received, or the results that they posted, were better or worse in the Tesseract schools than in the comparison schools. This may be because the courts had already awarded compensation to students who had not received all services due them. On the current assumption that inclusion programs can improve outcomes for special education students, the Maryland evaluators commended EAI

> for its success in cutting the number of students eligible for Level IV special education services, its mission to educate otherwise-segregated students in the regular classroom, and its efforts to eliminate the fragmentation of "pull-out" instruction through a full inclusion program for students needing special services. This aspect of the Tesseract program, if eventually judged successful, may be EAI's shining contribution to urban education.

However, the program was said to be in need of careful evaluation "to determine whether the students who would otherwise have been eligible for Level IV special education services have been well-served." This was particularly true since EAI had cut the number of students eligible for all special education services, which suggested that "students who should be receiving services are not."[59]

One side effect of the inclusion of Level IV special education services for the Tesseract schools should be noted: owing to the lower percentage of children eligible for Level IV services, a higher percentage of pupils' scores are reported for inclusion in the test result analysis.

Thus, with the exception of the proportion of pupils who are eligible for special education services, the overall similarity between the Tesseract and comparison schools is the most salient finding with respect to outcomes detailed in the evaluation report.

COSTS

The assessment of cost information is important for the overall interpretation of the findings from Baltimore. According to the evaluation report, EAI received $6,056 for each pupil in the Tesseract schools. It was permitted to use 7.5 percent of that amount, or $454, for "non-school costs."[60] Thus, the report indicates that EAI spent $5,602 per pupil at the school level, against an average of $4,973.50 for school-level costs in the comparison schools, a difference of 11.2 percent.[61] Note that it is possible that EAI used some of the school-level funding for central-office-type services. Unfortunately, the nonschool costs of the Baltimore City public schools are not reported in the evaluation.[62]

These data indicate that EAI had more resources to work with in the Tesseract schools than did the comparison schools. As stated in the evaluation,

> The promise that EAI could improve instruction without spending more than Baltimore City was spending on schools has been discredited. The exact level of difference between Tesseract and comparison schools in spending for the school-based costs has yet to be determined, although the difference between Tesseract and comparison schools for school-based costs will be 11.2 percent in 1995–96. Understandably, there is an expectation of visible and significant results for an increase in expenditure.[63]

If the company made some headway, then "11 percent more than the comparison schools is not an excessive price differential for significant school improvement efforts in a school system with a per-pupil spending level that is considerably lower than the average per-pupil spending in Maryland school systems."[64]

Although it is not possible to determine precisely where the additional resources were spent in the Tesseract schools, EAI used interns in its classrooms more than control schools used paraprofessionals or other adults. Observations indicate that an intern was present in Tesseract schools 84 percent of the time, while an assisting adult was present in the control-group schools 23 percent of the time.[65]

Finally, there are important cost-related issues not addressed in the evaluation report. Nothing indicates how much of the money received by EAI actually went into the schools and how much went to profit, a contentious issue in the privatization debate. Since only 1 page out of a 118-page report devoted to costs clearly detailed cost analysis, that was not part of this investigation. However, a recent report by the Government Accounting Office notes that, for the first two years of the contract, EAI reported gross profits of $1.9 million and $3.3 million respectively.[66]

PARENTAL VOICE

Choice was not one of the features of the EAI initiative. However, Tesseract's stated commitment was to parent involvement, and while six

Tesseract schools had full-time parent liaison staff in 1994–95, only three comparison schools did. The evaluation report developed a scale for assessing parental involvement that included thirteen categories and scored the schools based on interviews. The scale ranges from 0 (no activity) to 4 (fully functional activity), and each school's score was an average across the thirteen areas of parent involvement. Based on this research the evaluators concluded, "Despite the introduction of four new parent involvement activities into Tesseract schools, there appears to be little difference between parent involvement in Tesseract and comparison schools. . . ."[67] Even with parent liaison staff, EAI's program seemed to make little difference.

ACCOUNTABILITY

One of the effects of the privatization debate is that attention to school performance appears to increase in districts involved in experimentation. Clearly this has been the case in Baltimore, where local debates and press coverage of the EAI contract have reached a national audience.

A key claim of privatizers is that firms that undertake initiatives such as EAI's in Baltimore are willing to submit themselves to a direct test of their effectiveness that is not present in the typical public school arrangement: a contract is entered into with the express understanding that it will not be renewed if performance is unsatisfactory. If the UMBC evaluation report shows one thing, though, it is that even with a professional research approach, it is not simple to determine the beneficial or harmful effects of privatization initiatives. (For example, though the report found too much preparation for testing in *all* Baltimore schools, it is not clear whether being in the limelight had anything to do with this.) At a different level, the very fact that the school district must evaluate whether the privatization initiative has "worked" can lead to an increase in accountability; a detailed report such as the one prepared by UMBC, which provides information on all public schools in Baltimore, may not have been produced without the need to evaluate EAI.

There is another lesson in accountability derived from the EAI experience that was not appreciated sufficiently in the era of performance contracting. Education has multiple outcomes, and if an organization such as EAI is going to be judged on one or more of those in particular, then there will be strong incentives to effect change in that area more forcefully than in others, in order to present information that supports a continuation of the contract. For EAI, as well as for the Baltimore schools in general, test score changes have become paramount, eclipsing other teaching.

Another accountability issue is how money is spent. While UMBC researchers and Baltimore public school officials were able to track decreases in staffing as well as increases in computers in the Tesseract schools, EAI used its legal rights as a private firm to keep its financial books closed to scrutiny. The GAO reports that when they asked the company for documentation on expenses, EAI refused to provide it. Public institutions are often wracked by scandals about unwise or even illegal spending, but this is because their finances are open to public view. When private firms enter the world of services traditionally provided by government, the public loses out in terms of accountability.

EQUITY

Of its nine schools, the EAI initiative involved seven elementary schools, representative of Baltimore public elementary schools generally, and thus there are no macro-level equity issues involving school selection. For example, 85 percent of the students in the Tesseract schools qualified for free or reduced-price lunch compared to 86 percent of the pupils in the comparison schools. Moreover, because the EAI initiative did not turn over the entire district's management to a private company, and because it did not involve choice, there do not appear to be equity issues at stake.

One equity-related concern with privatization initiatives that include rewards based on test scores is that the contractor will concentrate on students near a particular cutoff score, where more apparent progress can be achieved. Assistance for students who are far below the cutoff, which would require greater efforts, might well be deemphasized as a consequence of the difficulty of raising their scores above the contractor's performance threshold. The independent evaluation does not discuss the issue of poorly performing students and does not present a special analysis of this subgroup.

Beyond this, it is important to recall that per-pupil spending for the Baltimore City Public Schools does not approach the levels common to surrounding suburban districts; in those districts, ample funding enables students to have both computers and high ratios of teachers to students. The narrow range of data comparing Tesseract with other Baltimore schools suggests that EAI's profits, garnered largely through substituting computers for teachers, did not harm (or help) Tesseract students. However, the most serious equity issue—that privatization may have exacerbated the differences between the urban and suburban schools—remained outside the study.

CONCLUDING FINDINGS ON BALTIMORE

The UMBC evaluation report is useful reading for anyone interested in recent privatization initiatives and the intricacies of educational evaluation.

Many of the evaluators' observations point out the similarities between the Tesseract and comparison schools rather than the differences. BCPS's broader reform efforts may well have affected all schools, rather than just the Tesseract schools. Or perhaps the Tesseract effort, which was seen as a radical alternative, spurred the entire system to action. But in most cases, the evaluator's positive findings reflected approaches to school revitalization in evidence wherever there is a genuine commitment to public school reform.

The following examples are taken directly from the evaluation report's final observations:

> The evaluation team found Tesseract and comparison schools more alike than different, and the researchers saw innovation in leadership and teaching in the comparison schools. The new managerial latitude for all Baltimore City schools was in evidence at the comparison schools, the visible level of maintenance was high, the chronic shortage of books and materials has been overcome by a substantial level of spending for instructional materials in the 1992–93 school year, formal staff development in comparison schools was, for most schools, at least as extensive as at Tesseract schools, and Chapter I monies and various school initiatives have brought considerable technology into Baltimore City elementary schools. . . . The less-than-complete success of EAI management of some Baltimore City schools does not mean that private management of public schools can not work. On the other hand, there have been lessons learned from this experience that can be applied without private management.[68]

Thus, in Baltimore, after three years of private sector management, the overall results more closely resembled the outcomes of other efforts at public school reform than they did some profoundly new conception of education. Moreover, a number of conclusions at least call into question the far-reaching claims of the outspoken privatization cheerleaders. For example:

> To date, the "management expertise" that the private sector should be able to bring to bear on a public enterprise has not been sufficient for the expected level of transformation of the Tesseract schools in Baltimore City. The evaluation team inferred inadequate strategic planning processes in a number of areas. . . . Computer-assisted instruction was sufficiently implemented in the Tesseract schools so that the . . . reading and integrated learning system was given a fair test of its effectiveness

in raising test scores. After two full years, the CTBS reading scores were not sufficiently improved to establish the success of the reading integrated learning system.[69]

THE DENOUEMENT

Even though it found positive points to make, the evaluation by the University of Maryland research team presented serious criticisms of privatization in Baltimore. At the same time as the report came out, the city of Baltimore was experiencing a financial shortfall that would necessitate cuts in school funding, and thus in payments to EAI.[70]

By the first two weeks of November 1995, negotiations between the city and the company were intense but shaky, with Mayor Schmoke threatening to end the EAI contract. A vociferous public meeting was held at city hall on November 20.[71] In the next few days, a tentative agreement was reached, which would have saved the city $7 million. But the agreement apparently left many details unresolved, and perhaps unresolvable.[72]

On November 22, Mayor Schmoke and members of the Baltimore school board announced jointly that the EAI contract would be terminated.[73] "We think we led the nation going into this," Superintendent Amprey said in an interview. "We can now probably give some lessons on how you sever from it."[74]

John Golle, EAI's chief executive, claimed to be "proud" of what the company had done. He also warned that the district would have to take over the $4–6 million leasing costs of EAI computers and other equipment "unless you want us to back up the truck and haul it away."[75]

CONCLUSION

In December 1995, the Maryland School Performance Assessment Program, which had tested grades 3, 5, and 8 statewide in the fall, released test results showing that, despite slight yearly gains (including EAI schools), scores in Baltimore City schools were lowest in the state.[76]

Does the EAI experience in Baltimore prove that a private company cannot produce educational results? Obviously not. Yet a number of complications contributed to the problematic nature of the EAI experience in Baltimore. While some can be avoided by other cities seeking to privatize, others appear inherent in the privatization process and thus more difficult to counteract.

First, the EAI contract, which was entered into with surprising haste, did not specify exactly how much test scores, attendance, or other educational outcomes were to improve with each year of the contract. Although both BCPS and the city were pleased with the physical changes in the Tesseract schools, there were no criteria for evaluating EAI in these and other areas, like accounting. Thus, no one—not EAI, nor the union, nor BCPS personnel, nor city officials, nor the evaluators—had clear benchmarks to assess progress and contract compliance.

Clearly, both Education Alternatives and districts throughout the country have learned from this difficult experience. However, while future contracts can be made more clear about performance criteria, such contracts will not resolve underlying issues of what is to be evaluated, and how to make more useful and accurate the evaluation of a company's effectiveness without inducing a narrowing of the objectives of the instruction offered merely to raising student test scores. EAI defined its Tesseract Way as a program stressing many of the most progressive ideas in education, from using hands-on activities and real life experiences as a basis for learning to encouraging group work through cooperative education and fostering students' different learning styles. However, all the student testing on which the company's effectiveness was judged was traditional in nature. Student portfolios and other forms of "authentic" assessment were never mentioned. There appears to be nothing in the EAI evaluation plan to encourage the development of these progressive educational methods in the Tesseract schools.

Second, EAI's cost-cutting measures focused on personnel. This has been the privatizers' key method of trimming budgets, and some school districts have clearly hoped that privatizers would wield a stronger arm against unions than they themselves have been able to. In Baltimore, EAI focused on two areas. It eliminated teaching and counseling positions. It also replaced classroom paraprofessionals with interns. Beyond the issue of apparent illegalities involved in the practice, EAI's method of mainstreaming special education students escaped rigorous evaluation. These methods could feed teachers' and parents' worst fears about what can happen to such students without appropriate supports and training of instructors.

EAI's attempts to remove all paraprofessionals in the classrooms, many of whom had years of experience and lived in the same neighborhoods as their students, may have alienated community constituencies as well as members of the Baltimore Teachers Union. Throughout the contract period, there was high turnover among the intern replacements, raising the question of whether the interns adequately filled the role of providing a second adult in the classroom.

Like other privatizers, Educational Alternatives, Inc., has sold its programming as yielding better results for lower costs than the public sector. In Baltimore, rather than saving money, EAI cost the city in excess of 11 percent more on the Tesseract schools than it spent on other BCPS schools. This is a significant difference in a city as financially strapped as Baltimore, particularly given the negligible improvement in academic performance.

If trimming the fat from urban school district budgets means spending on corporate travel, lawyers, and public relations consultants while cutting teachers and paraprofessionals and increasing class size, then even with the addition of computers it is unlikely that private companies can improve student achievement. Unions have fought for working conditions that have not always enhanced the education of students, but privatization aimed at union busting may offer neither instructional benefits nor financial savings to public education.

Finally, it is important to stress that EAI sought to make a profit in a district whose per-pupil spending was already at the bottom of its state's rankings. The next chapter turns to somewhat different stories, among them the Hartford experience, where EAI sought to improve education in a high-spending district.

5.

EXPERIMENTING WITH PRIVATIZATION

We decided to show how things can work.

Joseph Kellerman, founder of the
Chicago Corporate Community School[1]

Baltimore's experience with Education Alternatives, Inc., is among the most publicized attempts at privatization. But it is only one of the privatization models which cities and districts have experimented with since the late 1980s. These experiences have incorporated different kinds of regulation as well as variations in openness to public scrutiny; they have involved both parental choice arrangements and assignment to neighborhood schools; and they have included relationships between districts and both nonprofit and for-profit groups and institutions. Within the for-profit sector, some schools are owned and run for profit by a single individual,[2] others by a group of corporations, and still others by large companies like EAI that hope to franchise their educational product and offer stocks to shareholders. Nevertheless, together the experiments suggest some of the possibilities and problems with privatization as it affects student outcomes, school costs, parental voice, accountability, and equity.

THE CHELSEA-BOSTON UNIVERSITY PARTNERSHIP

JOHN SILBER (president, Boston University): *What I have told the school committee of Chelsea is that we're going to take something from you. We're going to take your right to engage in political patronage. . . . But we're going to give you something else, and that is the opportunity to be the public servants in the highest tradition, and you're going to have the opportunity of improving the schools of Chelsea and improving the lives of those children in Chelsea.*

ALBERT SHANKER (president, American Federation of Teachers): *I think it's a good proposal. And I think the one problem with it is that it's coming from outside, top down, which is contrary to every modern principle of management which says if you want something to work from the beginning, you start by involving all the people who are going to have to make it work.*

Exchange on ABC's *Nightline*, December 1, 1988.[3]

Chelsea, Massachusetts, across the Charles River from Boston, is a small, run-down urban community. While Horatio Alger graduated from Chelsea High School 140 years ago, today's students are largely from Latin America and Southeast Asia, and success stories are rare. By the late 1980s, at the time the Chelsea-Boston University Partnership was formed, the median household income in Chelsea was the lowest of any city in Massachusetts; more than 28 percent of Chelsea families were headed by single parents (about a fourth of all teenage girls were either pregnant or mothers), and nearly three-fourths of Chelsea's public school students were from families receiving public assistance.[4]

The Chelsea school district also has one of the poorest property tax bases in Massachusetts. In 1985, the district was on the brink of insolvency and required a $5 million interest-free loan from the state to maintain school services. At the onset of the partnership with Boston University, Chelsea's per-student spending on education was among the lowest in the state. In contrast to the popular image of bloated urban school bureaucracies, the Chelsea schools budget could not even provide administrative support to run the district, and so its fiscal operations were maintained by the city government.

Politically, the Chelsea school district was also troubled. None of the seven members of the Chelsea School Committee (school board) had children in the schools. Moreover, though students in the Chelsea schools were only 28 percent white (55 percent were Latino, 12 percent Asian, and 5 percent black), the seven board members were all white.[5] According to Glenn Jacobs, a sociologist studying the community, "Prior to the Boston University takeover of the public schools in 1989, Chelsea's Latino community, if not having slept through Chelsea's civic affairs, found itself more a hapless supplicant to the powerful than a respected player in city politics."[6]

In 1989, after two years of discussion between Boston University (BU) and the Chelsea School Committee, the management of the Chelsea schools was turned over to BU. (Belated opposition would come from the Latino community and the teachers' union, worried about BU president John Silber's anti-bilingual education and antiunion pronouncements.) Although called a partnership, the contract provided BU with nearly absolute authority. As the university's Education School dean Peter Greer put it, "We were going to take all the risks. Why shouldn't we have full control?"[7]

Boston University entered the Chelsea schools with a seventeen-point comprehensive plan for educational reform. Produced by approximately sixty Boston University faculty members under the direction of the School of Management, the plan included improving hiring procedures and increasing salaries and benefits for all Chelsea school staff, as well as correcting fiscal mismanagement. It also involved revitalizing the curriculum of the school system; providing professional development for teachers; creating before- and after-school programs for both students and adults; designing new forms of student assessment; and establishing procedures "which are of assistance in monitoring programs and which act as incentives for staff members in each school."[8] Acknowledging Chelsea's broader socioeconomic needs, the plan called for inclusive family schooling: education would be directed to all age groups, from prekindergarten through adults, and schools would provide health and social services. BU would devote considerable effort to an early childhood education program.

Much of the first year was spent developing a workable relationship between Boston University and the Chelsea community. Although BU created an independent fund-raising entity, A Different September Foundation, which raised $2.2 million for the project, funds were slow in coming and were insufficient to pursue all of the university's first-year goals. Nevertheless, to improve community relations, BU hired a new, Latino superintendent, Diana Lam, who quickly set about creating a variety of communication vehicles for teachers and parents. Curriculum objectives for grades k-5 were created; the Early Learning Center for preschool and kindergarten students was initiated; and a Parent Information Center as

well as a Health Care, Counseling and Coordination Center at the high
school were opened. A first-year implementation report by Pelavin
Associates argued that, while interaction between the School Committee
and the BU management team continued to be "problematic," a number
of changes indicated "progress toward an improved academic climate."[9]

The report, "Years Two and Three of the Chelsea-BU Partnership,"
issued in 1994, again by Pelavin Associates, remains the most up-to-date
comprehensive assessment of Boston University's involvement in the
Chelsea schools. A brief report, "Urban School Reform," was put out by A
Different September Foundation in the same year, but its purpose was to
highlight areas of accomplishment.[10] Therefore, the following analysis of
the relationship is based largely on the "Years Two and Three" report.

The 1994 Pelavin evaluation describes year two (1990–91) as "the
calm before the storm."[11] In April 1991, Chelsea voters failed to pass a
local override of Massachusetts' Proposition 2 1/2.[12] With a deficit of $9.5
million, the city government (and thus the school district) was forced
into receivership.

A month later, citing tensions with BU—"there were too many boss-
es"[13]—Superintendent Lam resigned to run for mayor of Boston. In her
stead, Boston University appointed Peter Greer, Dean of the School of
Education. Although he had been chair of BU's management team during
the first two years of the project, his appointment exacerbated community feelings that the university was proceeding unilaterally. Lam's Teacher
Board (a voluntary group of teachers who met to discuss issues of concern), monthly teachers' coffees, parent coffees, and parent newsletters,
were all cancelled with Greer's arrival. He would leave by the end of the
year, to be replaced by a third superintendent, John Gawrys, who committed himself to remaining throughout the ten-year Chelsea-BU
Partnership.

Receivership, which turned the Chelsea school district into a ward of
the state, also created a new layer of bureaucracy. The state receiver in
Chelsea had ultimate control of all educational decisions having fiscal
impact. In addition, the receiver could raise and impose fees, as well as
ignore union contracts.

The receivership, and a budget reduced by approximately 25 percent,
forced BU into a crisis-management mode, which entailed closing or reorganizing schools that had recently been restructured, decreasing or ending
promised programs, and laying off personnel. Many students and teachers
found themselves in a different school during each of the first three years.
Physical education, art, and vocational education were also eliminated or
scaled back, and several sixth- and seventh-grade classes grew as large as
forty-five students.

Among the layoffs, the most controversial was elimination of the bilingual education coordinator. Close to 70 percent of Chelsea students are not native English speakers. However, from the start of the Partnership the bilingual program had been a point of discord between the Latino community and the BU management team, because the latter maintained that the legal mandate governing the teaching of non-English speakers would best be met by teaching students English.

In the midst of program cuts and layoffs, Boston University enriched the preschool program, transforming it into a cornerstone of the Partnership; in addition, a music program was significantly expanded. While the 1994 evaluation describes these two decisions as being based on educational philosophy, it attributes others to space considerations, economic necessity, or "whim." The result was both a sense of "constant change and commotion" among teachers and students and a new surge of criticisms leveled at BU by many groups, including administrators, the Chelsea School Committee, students, and the community.[14]

Among the Partnership's many initiatives, the Chelsea High School Health Clinic was both the most successful and the most controversial. Run by the Massachusetts General Hospital/Chelsea Memorial Health Center in cooperation with Boston University's School of Public Health, the clinic opened in September 1990. A major focus of the clinic was helping new immigrant students with their special health problems. However, the clinic also became the center of a bitter debate during 1991–92, when the management team rejected a proposal to distribute condoms and the School Committee, with widespread community support, overrode the decision. The management team then delayed on stocking the condoms, so that they were not given out at all during the 1991–92 school year.[15]

Despite these and other continuing sources of disharmony, by the end of the third year, Pelavin Associates found several educational improvements in Chelsea. The Early Learning Center involved more preschool students each year and drew national attention. Two elementary schools had integrated compensatory education pull-out programs into the regular school day. The music program was emerging as one of BU's primary foci. As a result of the dropout prevention program, which involved a number of activities coordinated by its own director, the dropout rate was halved between 1988–89 and 1991–92. Despite the condom conflict, the Chelsea High School Health Clinic appeared to be a strong success. Professional development had been provided in math and other areas. The entire district moved to a trimester scheduling plan, which, while controversial among teachers and students, attracted the attention of educators nationwide.

The following discussion considers the effects of the Chelsea-Boston University Partnership in the five critical schooling categories.

OUTCOMES

In its proposal to Chelsea, Boston University promised quantifiable outcomes only after the fifth year. Moreover, the BU management team faced a series of unexpected crises beyond its control. Nevertheless, the publication of student results at the end of the third year caused widespread criticism of Boston University. According to "Years Two and Three of the Chelsea-BU Partnership," the dropout rate among Chelsea high school students was reduced from 18 percent to 7 percent during the first three years. (The dropout rate would rise again to 13 percent in 1993–94, although the increase was said to be due to school system efforts to reenroll students who had previously dropped out.)[16] Attendance, however, remained between 88 and 90 percent over the first three years. Students' basic skill test scores also had not improved since BU's arrival. (While the percentage of third graders passing the Massachusetts reading, writing, and mathematics basic skills tests increased between the 1988–89 and 1990–91 academic years, the percentage of sixth and ninth graders passing these tests fell.) In addition, SAT scores of Chelsea High seniors, which showed a slight increase during year two, plummeted during year three.

These, of course, are all traditional yardsticks; although Boston University had promised to develop more comprehensive measures of student performance, it had not done so. Moreover, while the Pelavin report noted progress in creating activities relevant to a number of BU's seventeen goals (such as health clinics and after-school programs), the university was not evaluating these critical areas.

"Years Two and Three of the Chelsea-BU Partnership" also observed that the arena in which BU had invested most of its energy and resources, sometimes at the expense of the middle- and high school years, was the early childhood program. In addition to the Early Learning Center, there were seventeen kindergarten classrooms (four of which were bilingual), a Chelsea Home Instruction Program for Preschool Youth (HIPPY), and a High Technology Home Daycare Project, which linked family day-care providers with educational resources outside their homes. However, BU had not evaluated the effects of this rich variety of programs.

COSTS

Although A Different September Foundation had fallen short of its fund-raising goals at the end of the third year, the Chelsea school district was helped financially by its partnership with BU. The foundation's revenue was particularly important during the town's years of financial crisis. Since the Chelsea-BU Partnership was neither an attempt to show how schools could be run for less money, cost-effectiveness may not be an issue. Yet one of the important strengths of the Partnership has been BU's awareness that tax revenues in a city like Chelsea are inadequate, and its willingness to assist with securing outside funding.

PARENTAL VOICE

Privatization in Chelsea has not involved any form of school choice. On the contrary, some students were forced to switch back and forth between schools during the first three years, as schools were restructured or closed for pedagogical, budgetary, or other reasons.

However, among the seventeen Boston University goals was establishing programs that link families and schools. The University did this in a variety of ways: through the HIPPY program for families of preschool children; a Parent Information Center; and a number of school-sponsored programs for parents. In addition, two parent outreach programs in Chelsea were started by BU faculty even before the onset of the Partnership, and continued throughout the evaluation period. The Intergenerational Literacy Project, which expanded during the first three years of the Partnership, attempted to improve the literacy of parents and grandparents as a way of enhancing students' language arts skills. Three times a year, the project offered eight-week sessions for marginally literate parents and others who care for children under the age of ten. The Adult Basic Education Program, which began in 1975, offered courses from basic literacy instruction to GED preparation. It was continuing under the Partnership, although largely independent of BU.

Though this assortment of programs clearly provided a number of opportunities for parents to improve their skills (and their capacity for parenting), in all these ventures parents remained in a passive, learning role. Their opinions and choices were not actively sought. One medium was developed to give parents and community members a voice in the Chelsea-BU Partnership—the Chelsea Executive Advisory Committee (CEAC). Created as the official vehicle through which the Chelsea community could respond to and influence BU's efforts, the CEAC was composed of representatives of fifteen community organizations. However, by the end of the third year, the CEAC remained no more than a "forum for dissent." Limited in its effectiveness because of "internal conflicts and a precarious relationship with the Management Team," in 1991 its very existence was questioned.[17]

ACCOUNTABILITY

The Chelsea School Committee relinquished its traditional responsibilities to the BU management team when it agreed to the Partnership. While it retained the authority to override outside management decisions by a two-thirds vote, in the first three years of the project, the School Committee only exercised this veto once—in the case of condom distribution, and even then its opposition could not overcome BU's delaying tactics.

As of 1994, none of the School Committee members had children in the Chelsea schools. However, as a result of the BU agreement, the community voted in one Latino member, a woman who supported "very few of BU's decisions and programs."[18] "Years Two and Three of the Chelsea-BU Partnership" describes BU as having made "only minimal headway" in engaging the community and summarizes the relationship as "one of strong, mutual distrust, resulting in Chelsea blaming BU for too many of the community's problems, and in BU excluding the community, even its elected officials, from the decision-making process." While the predominant feeling in Chelsea toward Boston University was one of "resentment," BU's attitude toward the community "remain[ed] one of 'father knows best.'"[19]

This paternalism affected (and infected) important accountability issues. A study of the BU-Chelsea relationship describes the university's early negotiation with the state of Massachusetts to run the school district. As a private institution, the university demanded exemption from state laws requiring open meetings and public records.[20] The state's Department of Education gave only a qualified endorsement of the Partnership. As its legal counsel pointed out, "It is hard to protect the prerogatives of a private institution such as BU and at the same time conform its conduct of public school business to the requirements that apply to school communities."[21] Although Boston University would acquiesce to some openness, the "Years Two and Three" evaluation indicates a continuing tendency for the university to resist public accountability, particularly toward the Chelsea community.

Receivership may well have exacerbated Boston University's paternalism toward Chelsea, while strengthening its sense of accountability to the state. As money was now controlled by the state, it was to Massachusetts that BU had to turn in its decisionmaking. Thus, not only was the Chelsea School Committee largely ignored, but so were ordinary parents and community members. As the Pelavin report argues: "If a goal of the partnership is to demonstrate how a school system 'should' be run, one must ask at what point in its proposed ten-year tenure in Chelsea the Management Team will see fit to incorporate and 'train' those who will be responsible once again for running the schools after BU's departure.[22]

The brief report by A Different September Foundation in no way refutes the paternalism of BU's management; however, in behalf of community support for the Partnership, it contends: "The elected Chelsea School Committee has the right to cancel the Partnership contract with Boston University at any time by a simple majority vote. The question has never been raised in five years."[23]

EQUITY

The influence of the Chelsea-Boston University Partnership on equity concerns appears mixed. For Chapter 1 (now Title I) students whose programming has been integrated into the regular classroom day, the Partnership has had a positive effect. For bilingual students and their families, who may have wanted classes in Spanish or Chinese, immersion English may not seem like a step toward equal educational opportunity. Some families have also complained that the preschool program has taken an undue proportion of resources, and that middle-school and high school students have been comparatively deprived. Through it all, and despite the best efforts of A Different September Foundation, students in the Chelsea school district have continued to attend schools funded at a much lower level than most schools in Massachusetts.

THE MILWAUKEE CHOICE PROGRAM

I doubt whether the current system of urban education can be reformed. I think it should ultimately be scrapped and replaced with a new system—essentially a voucher or choice system. We should give parents the purchasing power they need to enroll their children in any public or private, non-sectarian school that complies with essential standards.

Milwaukee mayor John O. Norquist [24]

The Milwaukee Public Schools serve 110,000 children; 70 percent are African-American. The public school dropout rate is a staggering 50 percent. In 1987, a survey of Milwaukee public school teachers found that 62 percent would not want their children to attend the school where they teach.[25]

The Milwaukee Choice Program began in 1990 as a way to help low-income students in Milwaukee's public schools attend private, nonsectarian schools in the city. (However, participating private schools are not required to enroll special education students.) The state provides approximately

$3,000 in tuition money for each student enrolled in the program, which is equivalent to the sum the Milwaukee public schools receive per student in state aid. The program has been limited to students from families living at or below 1.75 times the federal poverty level. Although enrollment cannot by local law exceed 1.5 percent of the total enrollment in the Milwaukee Public Schools, it has grown since the 1990–91 school year, when the program began with 341 students; 830 students participated in 1994–95,[26] and 1400 were part of the program in 1995–96.[27] In 1994–95 twelve private schools (out of twenty-three private, nonsectarian schools in Milwaukee) took part, an increase from seven in 1990–91. In 1995–96, seventeen private schools signed up with the program, although two ceased operation in February 1996, following a state audit.[28]

Unlike Baltimore's or Chelsea's privatization, which have involved no school choice, the goal of Milwaukee's program is to allow students to choose from a variety of private schools. Thus, it is also rare among the many choice programs in the United States, which are typically limited to public schools.

As important, no other choice program involving private schools has benefited from a consistent, independent evaluation. John Witte at the University of Wisconsin-Madison was selected as the independent evaluator for the Milwaukee Choice Program in September 1990. Since then the annual evaluations of Witte and his team have been funded almost exclusively through foundations and have received widespread coverage as well as several critiques.[29] The review that follows incorporates the major findings from the "Fourth-Year Report," which includes findings from the entire four years of the program.

OUTCOMES

The students who entered the Milwaukee Choice Program had poor public school records: most were near the bottom in academic achievement. To evaluate the Milwaukee Choice Program over its four-year time span, the evaluators compared the achievement test results for students in the program to all Milwaukee Public Schools students and to low-income, low-achieving Milwaukee public school students. As the report indicates, the latter group is the "most relevant" for comparisons.[30] Since choice students were low achievers, the important question is how much their scores changed over the four years. In fact, their scores varied "considerably" over this period:

> Choice students [sic] reading scores increased in the first year, fell substantially in the second year, and have remained approximately the

same in the third and fourth years. Because sample size was very small in the first year, the gain in reading was not statistically significant, but the decline in year two was. In math, choice students were essentially the same in the first two years, but recorded a significant increase in the third year, but that was followed by a significant decline this last year.[31]

In these and other ways, the Witte team found them to be like other low-income Milwaukee students:

> Regression results controlling for a number of factors and comparing choice students to MPS [Milwaukee Public Schools] show mixed and mostly insignificant results over the four years. Thus there is no systematic evidence that choice students do either better or worse than MPS students once we have controlled for gender, race, income, grade, and prior achievement.[32]

> The key test . . . is the longitudinal effect of being in the Choice Program. . . . The results, unfortunately, do not provide a consistent pattern.[33]

A secondary analysis of Witte's data by scholars at the University of Houston and Harvard University contests these findings, and argues that those students in the choice program for three or more years made significant progress in reading and math, and substantially outperformed Milwaukee Public School control students.[34] However, the validity of the comparison methodology has also been challenged.

In comparing attendance records, the Witte team found the differences between the choice students and those in the Milwaukee Public Schools to be "slight" and varied over the four years of the study.[35]

The Witte team considered attrition by choice students to be the most troubling aspect of the program. Excluding students who had to leave the private school that closed during the first year, attrition over the first three years was 40 percent, 35 percent, and 31 percent respectively. The average of these figures was judged to be about twice that of the Milwaukee Public Schools, although the evaluators believed that the rates were a "problem" for students in both settings.[36]

COSTS

The Milwaukee Public Schools' average expenditure per pupil is well above the amount paid to the private schools for each pupil in the Choice

Program. The Milwaukee Choice Program pays the participating private schools the "equivalent to the Milwaukee Public School (MPS) per-member state-aid (estimated to be $3,209 in 1994–95) . . . in lieu of tuition for the student."[37] Yet in 1990–91, the per-pupil general revenue earmarked for the Milwaukee Public Schools from all sources was $6,638, composed of $555 from federal agencies, $2,384 from local sources (almost entirely local taxes), and $3,700 from the state of Wisconsin.[38]

What is not known is the full costs to the private schools of educating Milwaukee Choice pupils. Tuition and fees in 1993–94 at the private schools involved varied from $1,080 to $4,000. "For five of the tuition-charging schools, the choice voucher of $2,987 is at least a break even amount relative to tuition charges. For three schools the voucher represents a net loss compared to tuition."[39]

The Milwaukee Public Schools have also contracted with private schools for the education of at-risk students, at a cost of "approximately $2,000 more revenue per pupil than the choice payments."[40] This has led some schools to balance the number of choice and contract students and raises the possibility of some students being supported by both programs.

Finally, a succession of private school closings during the course of the project raises questions about the economic viability of the participating private schools. While a school closed during the first year because of financial problems (leaving students stranded at midyear), the most recent closing of two schools in February 1996 was prompted by a state audit showing that the schools had inflated their enrollment figures and received more state funds than they were entitled to.[41]

PARENTAL VOICE

For all four years, the most positive outcome for Choice Program students was the satisfaction level expressed by their parents:

> Parental satisfaction with the private schools dramatically exceeded satisfaction with prior MPS schools. . . . Another indication of parent satisfaction is the grade parents give for their children's school. . . . For the four-year period, the average prior grade (on a scale where an A is 4.0) improved from 2.4 for prior MPS schools to 2.9 for current private schools. The overall grades have been relatively consistent for each year and always above the grades given to prior MPS schools.[42]

The Milwaukee Choice Program has given parents of poor children an option that they previously could not enjoy: enrollment in a private, non-sectarian school. Parents' perceptions of better "educational quality," "teaching approach and style," and "disciplinary environment and general atmosphere" in the private schools were the most important reasons for participation in the Choice Program.[43] Less important was dissatisfaction with the Milwaukee Public Schools, although parents in the Choice Program generally reported frustration with the public school system.[44]

Consistent with other research on parents who "choose to choose," the four-year analysis showed that parents who decided to enroll their child in the Choice Program were more likely to have been active in their child's education.[45] Their involvement was measured by a number of variables, including frequency of parents being contacted by schools, or of parents contacting schools, or of parental activity in school organizations and activities. In addition, choice parents showed significantly more involvement in their children's education at home through such activities as helping them with homework and reading with them. Once enrolled in the Choice Program, their high level of involvement was likely to continue and even to intensify.[46]

Whatever the benefits to the students involved in the Choice Program, the advantages conferred by these active parents were lost to the Milwaukee Public Schools. As the Witte evaluation argues, these same parents, if they had remained with the public schools to which their children had been assigned, might well have exercised "considerable influence in attempting to improve those" institutions. "Parents are educated, angry, involved, and have high expectations for their children. If engaged, and given the opportunity, they could push the public system rather than leaving it."[47]

ACCOUNTABILITY

The Milwaukee Choice Program has established accountability primarily by giving parents and their children the ability to select their schools. One of the downsides of such a system is the possibility that a private school in the program may fold, and students would lose critical education time by being forced to change schools again. This is exactly what occurred in the first year of the Milwaukee Choice Program:

> The operation and closing of the Juanita Virgil Academy was the most troublesome aspect of the first year of the Milwaukee Parental Choice Program. There are those who would argue that the failure of that school is to be expected in a market system of education. Whether one believes that that expectation outweighs the fact that approximately 150 children essentially lost a year's education is a value issue that we cannot resolve. Whatever one's values are, the price was high for those families involved.[48]

For such a choice program to work, information on the schools needs to be available to support informed choices. The private schools in the Milwaukee program do not have to meet the same performance assessments and standards as the Milwaukee Public Schools. "The Fourth-Year Report" recommends that the Choice Program schools essentially meet the same standards as the public schools. Moreover, it calls for better reporting on the part of the Choice Program schools to the Wisconsin Department of Public Instruction.[49] Finally, the recommendations propose a governance system with a board that has some outsiders and a requirement that all schools have their finances externally audited with a report available to the public.[50]

EQUITY

The Milwaukee Choice Program was created to serve the district's poorest children: those whose family income does not exceed 1.75 times the nationally defined poverty level. "In terms of reported family income, the average income [in the Choice Program] was $11,780 in the first four years." Accounting for inflation, applicants in 1993–94 were even poorer than the four-year average.

Although the students have been from low-income families and tend to be underachievers, the schools in the Choice Program have not been required to serve disabled students as in the Milwaukee Public Schools; the schools were "exempted by court ruling from the Education for All Handicapped Act."[51]

THE CHICAGO CORPORATE COMMUNITY SCHOOL

The CEO hires executives called "teachers." And they work on a product called "students." The bottom line is student achievement, as measured by the same tests used by the public schools.

Joseph Kellerman, founder of the
Chicago Corporate Community School[52]

In September 1988, after a year of preparation and study, the Corporate Community Schools of America (CCSA) opened in a former Catholic school in Chicago's North Lawndale, an inner-city neighborhood serving predominantly African-American and Hispanic students. Led by seventy-year-old Joseph Kellerman, chief executive officer of a Chicago firm of chain stores and once a resident of North Lawndale, the CCSA was a not-for-profit coalition of business executives, community leaders, and concerned educators. With sixteen major corporations providing full support for the school, the Chicago Corporate Community School was an attempt to provide a model for inner-city public schools by demonstrating replicable instructional methods, sound school management principles, and other "market-driven" innovations.[53] As an observer commented in 1990, Mr. Kellerman wanted to create schools that would be part of a research and development approach "as used to improve products."[54] This R&D approach featured an early intervention program, an emphasis on parental involvement in children's learning, and an arrangement to make the school the center of a network of support agencies to help students and their families.[55]

Although the Corporate Community School was an elementary school, enrollment started with two-year-olds, and went as far as age eight. The student body was selected at random from a large pool of applicants; out of 1,000 applicants, 150 students were accepted the first year. The school operated year-round, except for three weeks in August, and was open from 7 A.M. to 7 P.M. daily, providing breakfast, lunch, and snacks to its students. A full-time nurse-social worker acted as coordinator for a variety of services for parents.[56]

Although CCSA intended to show the efficiency of business by running the school on the same per-pupil budget as the public schools, its principal received a higher salary than did counterparts in the public school system, and the year-round schedule resulted in teachers' salaries being 10 percent higher than in the public school system. In addition, teachers were to garner raises based on students' performance. Thus, the first-year Corporate Community School costs were said to be "close to $5,000 per pupil," compared to $4,236 in Chicago and $4,480 across Illinois.[57]

To involve parents in learning, they were allowed to ride the bus with their children, to have lunch with them, and to participate in school activities. In addition, all parents were required to visit their children's teachers four times a year. The school also offered GED classes and programs in adult literacy and word processing.

In contrast to the Chicago public schools, however, which were moving governance closer to parents, the eleven-member board of directors of the Chicago Corporate Community School reserved only one place for a parent. Under the philosophy that "school governance should be placed in the hands of well-paid professionals," five members of the board of directors were "executives with proven expertise in finance, real estate, personnel, and management."[58] Three were "well-respected educators," and two were residents of the community.[59] In other words, like the Chelsea-Boston University Partnership, the Chicago Corporate Community School believed in its expertise and took a paternalistic stance toward the families it was serving.

A first-year progress report noted the following accomplishments: parents had become more involved in their children's learning, and opportunities had been provided for parents' own educational development. A program had connected families with social service agencies.

A second-year report in 1992 cited higher test scores among Chicago Corporate Community School students than among students in the Chicago public schools.[60] The various family services offered, as well as the longer school year, were assumed to be major contributors.

However, behind the good news, the CCSA was experiencing a good deal of turmoil. The school was supposed to develop "self-motivated children who are able to learn despite obstacles imposed by their living conditions."[61] Among the staff, some did not have adequate preparation as teachers, and some believed that the low achievement levels of African-American and Latino children were the result of a "conspiracy" in which compensatory education and other special services reinforced exactly the sense of failure they were set up to prevent. Thus, the school made little provision for children with special learning difficulties. Instead, in an effort to foster educational innovation, teachers ordered materials and planned curriculum in isolation, and there was little continuity from one level to the next.[62]

The school soon lost its first principal; indeed, there would be three principals in six years, and teacher turnover was quite high.

In 1992, after three years of operation, corporate financial support began to dwindle, and the Corporate Community School began looking for an alternative source of funding. In 1993, subsequent to a vote by the Chicago Board of Education, the Chicago Corporate Community School became the first private school to be integrated into the public school system. However, the corporations that had been involved committed to providing $700,000 in additional funds for the next five years. Although one staff member believes that the school has experienced "the chilling effect" of Chicago's public school bureaucracy, the addition of corporate contributions has enabled the school to continue several of its critical features, including year-round service, a twelve-hour day, a preschool program, instructional aides in every classroom, and social services provided centrally at the school.[63]

HARTFORD AND EAI

Probably the greatest contribution EAI will bring to Hartford . . . is a sense of accountability. Our school district, and most other school districts, hold neither students nor employees to high performance standards. It must happen for

both groups, but it begins with management—the school board, superinten-
dent, and private management—being held to high performance expecta-
tions, too.

Kathy Evans and Ted Carroll,
Hartford School Board members[64]

Hartford's experience with Education Alternatives, Inc., which
spanned only eighteen months, did not generate a formal evaluation.
Thus, its short history must be told through newspaper articles.

Hartford, a city of 140,000 with a large poor and minority population,
has thirty-two public schools serving approximately twenty-five thousand
students. Two-thirds of the children live in poverty, and one-third attend
bilingual or special education classes. Scores on standardized tests are
among the lowest in the state.

In March 1994, the district was in its fourth year of a fiscal crisis,
which forced it to cut programs and downsize.[65] As the *New York Times*
put it, "school supplies were so scarce that many teachers bought their
own. Buildings were in disrepair."[66] Although Hartford spent more per
pupil ($8,500) than most Connecticut communities, a higher proportion
was used for salaries and benefits. Teacher retirement benefits were costing the city $37 million per year, one-sixth of the district's spending.
The public school system spent far less on books and supplies than its
neighbors.[67]

In spring 1994, Hartford entered into discussions with EAI about privatizing its entire school system. During the summer, amidst warnings
from the American Federation of Teachers and a temporary injunction
by the union local against going forward, the school board began "ham-
mering out a deal" with EAI.[68] The city council opposed the relationship
with EAI, as did the superintendent, Dr. Eddie L. Davis. Although the
school board was divided, the majority favored the proposed agreement. As
a member argued, "We are absolutely convinced that the current way of
operating does not work and cannot work."[69]

A pro forma competitive bidding process was staged, with the teachers' union offering one of the alternate bids. But by August an agreement
was worked out with EAI, and in early October the board voted six to
three to approve a five-year contract. Through this contract, which was
signed in November 1994, Hartford became the first city in the nation to
turn over all of its public schools to a private firm.

In accordance with the terms of the district's contract with EAI, the
company was to bring in its partners, KPMG Peat Marwick, Johnson
Controls, and Computer Curriculum Corporation, under the umbrella of
the Alliance for Schools that Work. The agreement stipulated that:

1. EAI would take charge of the entire Hartford school district and would "jump-start" the endeavor by investing $14 million of its own money in classroom and office technology.

2. EAI would spend about $1.6 million immediately to repair, secure, and upgrade school buildings.[70]

3. EAI would manage the district's budget of approximately $171 million, pay all bills, then take as profit what was left at the end of each year.[71]

4. EAI would assist Hartford in making both teachers and students accountable to higher performance standards.

5. EAI would supply improved purchasing, reporting, and data collection systems and would assist in developing new curriculum, as well as provide its own Tesseract programs to schools that wanted it.[72]

Because the company's takeover of the city's schools had been opposed by both the city council and the union, EAI pledged to avoid layoffs, honor union work rules, and use local contractors whenever possible. Nor would EAI have control over the retirement fund, which was part of the city council's budget. Important decisions, such as how EAI was to be paid and exactly how much control it would have, were left to a special contract negotiations committee.[73] A board member who had voted against letting in EAI said, "It's going to be one helluva year here."

Beyond its numerous uncertainties and loopholes, the terms of the contract were not particularly advantageous to the company. However, part of EAI's corporate strategy in Baltimore and elsewhere had been to list school district budgets as revenue, hoping to attract new stock investors through showings of strong growth. In addition, a contract in Hartford would demonstrate that the company could manage entire districts as well as individual schools.

EAI IN HARTFORD: THE FIRST YEAR

EAI began by spending $1.6 million of its own money on school repairs and painting, as well as photocopiers and walkie-talkies. By March 1995, two Hartford schools had computer labs capable of running the SuccessMaker curriculum, and a *Hartford Courant* story described the rapid cleanup of schools and distribution of supplies and computers.[74]

However, outfitting the remainder of Hartford's schools with the computers and wiring necessary for the SuccessMaker curriculum proved to be a problem. Although the plan was to avoid entirely rewiring old buildings by creating computer laboratories instead of installing computers in every classroom, some schools were so crowded that they had no room for labs.[75] Moreover, conflicts were beginning to arise with school principals who were loyal to Apple computers when EAI wanted to bring in IBMs.

Hartfords' financial morass soon became a new problem for the company: EAI had to help the city cover a $3.3 million budget shortfall. It also found that the district was losing $8 million per year on a recently approved early-retirement plan. In March, William Goins, EAI's chief operating officer in Hartford, told CEO John Golle, "These people don't plan to pay you. They say they do, but I don't believe them. They won't take any actions that substantiate their positions."[76] That same month, EAI's financial officer, Gary Franzi, was ignored when he presented the school board with his plan for taking over the payroll and all expenditures, which EAI saw as the key to finding the necessary budget savings. The school board said it had no money for the new accounting systems EAI wanted and told EAI it would have to put up the money itself. According to the contract, EAI was supposed to pay the bills and payroll out of its own funds—as much as $15 million per month—and submit vouchers for reimbursement. The company maintained that the contract had also specified that Hartford would first turn over all of its education budget authorization to EAI. Yet Superintendent Davis was allowing administrators to continue making purchases without going through EAI.

In April, Davis submitted a 1995–96 budget that included no money for any EAI initiatives. Even the computers and equipment the company had already leased were not covered. "In a district that is so needy, you can't decide that the only game in town is what you want, focusing on technology and putting more computers in," he said.[77]

Chastising the superintendent, the school board directed EAI to work cooperatively with Davis to draft an alternative budget. Instead, the company worked alone on a budget that would cover all its initiatives and yield a 3 percent profit. Its budget eliminated 220 teachers and 100 other employees and shifted as much as $15 million from salaries to additional computer labs. It also included a plan to decentralize radically the power of the schools administration by empowering local schools to make their own curriculum and expenditure decisions.[78]

The EAI budget was opposed by Superintendent Davis, and more than one thousand Hartford teachers staged a protest at a board meeting.[79] Justifying the proposed overhaul, EAI chief Golle compared Hartford to a cancer patient receiving chemotherapy. "We were hired to do a most unpleasant task, a task they obviously could not do alone—or they would have."[80]

By the end of May 1995, while the superintendent and EAI officials were still trying to piece together a workable budget, the school board decided to allocate nearly $5 million less to the district than had been expected.[81] However, at the insistence of Hartford's Mayor Michael Peters, it restored $3.3 million to the budget for equipment leases and accounting services already initiated by EAI.

In June 1995, the Hartford School Board voted seven to two to reduce EAI's direct role to five or six schools (the number varies according to the source of the report);[82] these were sites where the company had made progress in building computer labs and wiring classrooms for computer network systems. Additional schools within the district were to be phased in as "the situation permits."[83] The decision was attributed to protests by parents and teachers against the layoffs and cost slashings that would have resulted from full implementation of EAI's plans.[84]

In the next few months, arguments between the school board and EAI over finances continued. The contract said that EAI's expenses and profit would be paid out of the savings generated by greater efficiency. But since there were no savings, Golle insisted that expenses be paid out of the operating budget.

EAI IN HARTFORD: YEAR TWO

In the fall 1995 Hartford School Board elections, three new members were voted in, shifting the balance from five to four in favor of EAI to seven to two against.[85] Baltimore's cancellation of its contract with the company in November also left the school board shaken, and the resignation of several EAI executive officers further contributed to the general climate of uncertainty.[86]

On December 29, with the company threatening to leave Hartford by December 31 if it was not paid, the school board finally voted to compensate EAI $3 million for educational programs spelled out in the contract. Left unresolved was an additional $3.9 million the company claimed it was owed.[87] According to the city, this was supposed to come from savings that EAI had promised to achieve through more efficient management.[88] However, EAI threatened to close the computer labs it had installed in five schools and remove equipment unless it was paid this additional money.[89]

As in Baltimore, the school district's purse strings were largely controlled by the municipal government, and opposition among city council members continued as the company attempted to renegotiate its arrangement with the public schools. By January 1996, the school board realized that it was impossible to change the contract in a way that was mutually acceptable, and on

January 23 it voted seven to two to cancel the contract with EAI. The company had by then spent $11.5 million of its own money in the city.[90]

EAI reacted to the contract cancellation by threatening to sue Hartford and remove its equipment. The district then barred EAI and its subcontractors from entering schools where it had installed computers and other hardware. However, two weeks later, Mayor Peters said that Hartford might keep EAI on to oversee the finances of the school district; this strategy would help to ameliorate the legal dispute with the company and perhaps assist in solving the city's chronic budgetary problems.[91]

By late May, an agreement had been reached in which Hartford agreed to pay EAI $2.75 million to keep computers in five schools; other issues were still being negotiated.[92] At the same time, Superintendent of Schools Davis resigned, and the city council voted to ask the state for assistance in running Hartford's schools.[93]

CONCLUSION

The privatization experiments described here may seem too disparate for generalization. Yet the targets of all these privatization experiences were fiscally strapped urban school districts serving largely low-income students of color. Each experiment aimed to lower district spending while raising student achievement as measured by standardized test scores.

Although parents appear pleased with the Milwaukee Choice Program, and the dropout rate has been lowered in Chelsea, among these four experiments only the Chicago Corporate Community School, now defunct, and perhaps the Milwaukee Choice Program have generated improvements in achievement.

Except for the Choice Program in Milwaukee, these experiments also appear to place parents in a passive role. Moreover, all four experiments had difficulty in conveying information to families. While the Milwaukee program may yet overcome this problem, it will likely be difficult to obtain critical information from private schools lacking the same requirements for public dissemination or fiscal transparency as public agencies.

These privatization experiments have also created additional layers of bureaucracy. In Chelsea, the two extra institutional layers—the university and state receivership—brought in new decisionmakers that further distanced families from schools. In both Baltimore and Hartford, EAI's management team was added to the cast of decisionmakers, which already included the school board, the superintendent, and middle managers.

Although the Milwaukee Choice Program lowered costs for the school district, the amounts paid per pupil may not reflect the actual price of educating these students. None of the other projects described in this chapter saved money for public school districts. Even had EAI been able to lower costs in Hartford, the company would have taken half the savings in profits. On the other hand, Boston University stands out in this context, for rather than walking out during a budget crisis, as a for-profit company might have been forced by shareholder demands to do, the university stayed in Chelsea and attempted to manage the cutbacks and layoffs that have become routine for most urban districts.

Finally, the equity results of these projects are mixed: some students gained through choice programs and other expanded opportunities, others lost, either through reduced services or services not delivered at all.

"Pioneers get all the arrows," contends Michael Moe, who tracks for-profit education for the investment firm Lehman Brothers. This may be so.[94] But if privatization's results remain as spotty as current efforts indicate, its benefits will mostly inhabit the realm of ideology.

6.

PUBLIC EDUCATION IN TRANSITION

If schools are the vessels of our future, they are also the workshops of our democracy. . . . Public schools are not merely schools for the public, but schools in publicness: institutions where we learn what it means to be a public.
Benjamin R. Barber, Walt Whitman Center for the Culture and
Politics of Democracy, Rutgers University[1]

In the polarized images of public and private education created by privatization advocates, public school systems are portrayed as rigid, unresponsive, inefficient, and ineffective bureaucracies that provide poor-quality education and yield low student achievement. In the view of most privatizers, public schools severely limit parental participation and choice; fail dismally at holding themselves accountable to parents, citizens, or taxpayers; and, in spite of a welter of legal and procedural requirements, are unable to produce equity in resources or equity of opportunity for disadvantaged students.

Despite the ideological bias of these charges, they have a strong grounding in reality. Too many urban systems graduate too few students, and many of these graduates possess only eighth-grade skills. Urban systems are often run by large bureaucracies whose cumbersome accountability mechanisms are unresponsive to individual students' needs.[2] Many schools still limit access to parents and community constituencies.[3] And, some forty years after *Brown v. Board of Education*, our public education system still generates disparities in resource allocation and academic performance that favor already privileged students while compounding the disadvantages of students of color.[4]

But public schools have also worked to alter some of their unfair and restrictive organizational practices. This chapter explores how American public education is changing in response to escalating national criticism by those who want to preserve public education through substantial reform as well as by those who seek to privatize it. The examination focuses on the five categories used throughout this study: outcomes; costs; parental voice; accountability; and equity.

OUTCOMES

Given the focus of news coverage, it sometimes seems that the only mandate of public schools is to keep students in class and improve their test scores. Yet Americans obviously want much more from schooling than warehousing students or imparting the narrowly honed set of basic skills measured by standardized testing. We want to cultivate real literacy: the enjoyment of reading and the curiosity to discover and continue learning. We want to ensure our children's physical and mental health. We want to prepare students to make choices that enhance their chances in life and to become productive citizens. And we want young adults to take a variety of responsible roles that ensure their communities' well-being.

Given this wider vision of education, it seems indefensible to concentrate solely on dropout rates and test scores. Nevertheless, this is the narrow view on which the privatizers have focused their promises. It is also the measure used to demonstrate that America's schools, particularly in urban areas, fail their students.

Arguments about the failure of public education usually cite dramatic dropout rates from urban high schools, declining scores on the College Board's Scholastic Aptitude Tests (SAT) or the American College Testing (ACT) program, the poor performance of American students in comparison with those from other nations, or the disappointing results of students sampled in large-scale tests such as those conducted by the National Assessment of Educational Progress (NAEP).

Such statistics can make grim reading, especially when they are presented without the context necessary to suggest that the reality is more complex. Consider the concern about dropout rates, for example. Although some high schools have dropout rates approaching 80 percent of their entering student cohort, the national dropout rate is lower than it ever has been. Put differently, more Americans currently graduate high school than at any time in our history; in 1994, almost 76 percent of students graduated from their high schools.[5] In fact, only in the mid-1950s did

the nation's high school completion rate reach 50 percent, and it has been
rising steadily since then.[6]

But these nationwide statistical data mask a bifurcating system characterized by very high graduation rates in most suburban districts and
small towns and unacceptably severe dropout rates in many urban districts, particularly those serving students of color. Still, both African-
American and Latino dropout rates have been falling sharply during the
past two decades.

Though the drop in SAT scores of about 70 points from 1963 to 1975
has been cited as proof that American educational quality is declining,
scores have actually been increasing during the past decade. Moreover,
the enormous expansion of the SAT test-taking pool to include significant
percentages of poor and disadvantaged students complicates the supposed
deterioration in SAT results. If current SAT scores are compared with
those of fifty years ago, the 10.1 percent scoring more than 650 on the
verbal subtest in 1992 were majority female, of mixed socioeconomic status and racial classification, and from varied language backgrounds; the
6.68 percent who scored better than 650 in 1941, in contrast, were over-
whelmingly a white, male, northeastern elite.[7] Although the performance
of students of color still lags behind that of white students, the gap, as
measured by a wide variety of standardized tests as well as the NAEP, has
diminished across the past half-century. A recent National Science
Foundation report indicates that student achievement in science and
math, according to the NAEP, has increased since 1977. But improvements are especially marked among African-American and Latino students; the percentage of African-Americans attaining an acceptable
proficiency level in math, for example, went from 29 percent in 1978 to 51
percent in 1992.[8]

An important Rand study dispatches another frequent claim by privatization advocates—that much of the increased funding spent on compensatory education for disadvantaged students since the 1960s has failed
to produce positive results. Using NAEP data, this study demonstrates
that not only has the aggregate achievement of black and Latino students
moved closer to that of white students, it has increased far more than
would have been predicted after controlling for changes in family income
and family composition that directly affect student performance. The study
hypothesizes that Title I interventions have contributed significantly to
these gains.[9]

According to recent research, the monochromatic picture of
American public school failure when compared to schools in other
countries may also be misleading. American nine-year-olds read better
than anyone in the world except Finnish nine-year-olds, and American

fourteen-year-olds come almost as close, according to studies by the International Association for the Evaluation of Educational Achievement.[10]

Nevertheless, all international comparisons are problematic, since cross-country achievement studies often match up different categories of students. When, for example, the graduates of the almost universal American high school system are compared to the graduates of countries in which secondary school education is reserved for a relatively small elite, the test scores of American students will predictably be lower.[11] The crucial distinction is in the composition: American public education consistently produces a broadly inclusive pool of graduates because it is still among the most effective mass education systems that western industrialized nations have developed.[12]

Yet within our mass system, with its guarantee of universal access, American education has also produced educational tracks that lead to very divergent levels of achievement. A recent comparison of American and Japanese algebra students shows that the top 50 percent of American students score higher than their Japanese counterparts. But while Japanese students' results tend to fall within a narrow band, Americans exhibit an increasingly wide range of achievement as their schooling progresses.[13]

Thus, the problem facing American education is not simply that it has fostered unacceptably low levels of achievement, but that there are gross disparities between students who do relatively well and students who do poorly. The top third of U.S. students can compete effectively with the students of other countries. However, despite some gains across recent decades, the bottom third, which is predominantly poor, of color and the target of most privatization experiments, still suffers from dangerously low expectations and accomplishments.[14] Worse, unlike European systems that spend money throughout their highly differentiated systems, ours allocates significant societal resources to our college-bound tracks but very little to school-to-work tracks, the path taken by approximately half of all our public school graduates.[15]

What must be changed so that all our students, not simply the elite or the college-bound, receive an effective education? In 1983, A Nation at Risk initiated the latest wave of attacks on public education; at the same time, it argued that equity considerations should no longer drive school reform. In the subsequent years, several commentators suggested that America could not provide quality education for all students and recommended an overt triage approach.[16] But in the 1990s the pendulum has returned to an affirmation that "all children can learn," as well as to a new scrutiny of tracking and other systems of differentiation that contradict this rhetoric.[17]

IMPROVING OUTCOMES FOR ALL STUDENTS: THE DEBATE ABOUT SCHOOL REFORM

There are two current schools of thought about how to improve schools so that all children will learn: setting high standards that schools must then reach, and reforming the nation's public education system through changing one school at a time. Standards proponents argue for comprehensive benchmarks in core disciplines, curriculum frameworks based on those benchmarks to guide teaching, and assessment systems to help schools continuously reorganize and critique their instruction.[18] Advocates of bottom-up reform urge that schools try out a variety of organizational and instructional approaches and that teaching be individualized to meet the needs of students with a variety of learning styles. They argue that untracking American classrooms requires both culturally sensitive instruction that engages all students and nonstandardized assessments that respond to individual students' needs.[19] Simply setting standards, they point out, may well increase the extent of failure among students denied adequate opportunities to learn.

The debate that has emerged regarding standards versus bottom-up reform is critical to how we reshape American education. Each approach requires considerable conceptual, structural, and fiscal commitment. The effort involved in building a standards-based system is so substantial that it demands both a state-by-state and a national consensus. Yet a 1995 American Federation of Teachers study found that only thirteen states had developed standards clear enough to be used as part of a formal curriculum.[20] On the other hand, efforts to launch one-school-at-a-time change have strained the resources of national reform organizations such as the School Development Program, Accelerated Schools, and the Coalition of Essential Schools, forcing all these groups to shift their strategy from supporting individual member schools to developing regional assistance and support centers and other "scaling up" strategies.[21]

That the debate is being waged in Congress and state legislatures, in national forums called by industrialists and governors, and in school boards and faculty rooms throughout the nation demonstrates one of the critical strengths of the public sector. This is the terrain on which arguments about how to organize schooling for the next generation must take place.[22]

Unsurprisingly, this debate has escaped the privatizers. Neither comprehensive standards nor reform from below are central to their conception of how education should work. Nor do privatizers engage the issue of how our highly tracked, unevenly performing, and differentially funded public school system must be reorganized so that poor and disadvantaged children do indeed learn. Rather, many privatization advocates appear uninterested in the complicated details of schooling and educational reform. Like

Chubb and Moe, they argue that "the market *all by itself* has the capacity to bring about the kind of transformation that, for years, reforms have been seeking to engineer in a myriad of ways."[23]

CREATING THE NECESSARY SUPPORTS FOR LEARNING

With notable exceptions, such as the Chicago Corporate Community School and the Chelsea-Boston University Partnership, privatizers have also avoided the increasing need to link schooling with social support for children and families. As more of the nation's children grow up in deeper and more long-lasting poverty, the deprivation they bring to school increases.[24] The school systems serving these children must provide a growing range of nonacademic services. Breakfast and lunch programs, health clinics, education about substance abuse and pregnancy prevention—all these help create the preconditions for learning and the potential for normal development in thousands of stressed communities.[25] These services are costly, not only in dollars, but in terms of the time, energy, and attention they drain from the traditional tasks of schooling. Yet public schools are continually forced to weigh these services against their primary instructional mission.[26]

The past two decades have also witnessed a burst of immigrants from Latin American and Asian countries on the scale of the great waves of immigration from southern and eastern European countries in the late nineteenth century.[27] The special needs of the children of these new arrivals, many of whom have had little or no previous formal education, have prompted schools, particularly in urban areas, to develop new forms of language instruction as well as new, more culturally responsive teaching and support systems.[28]

Debates about the extent of the public schools' responsibility to meet student and family needs, to respond to immigrant and minority languages and cultural diversity, to provide education about sexuality, AIDS, violence, and substance abuse often monopolize attention and polarize communities. Yet these debates are critical exercises in any democracy. Unlike the private sector, public education cannot avoid open discussion about the challenge of shaping the next generation of citizens.

COSTS

Privatization advocates attack public education for maintaining an inefficient monopoly over teaching and school system operations. Because they believe that market mechanisms are less expensive, they maintain that more widespread use of contracting out and other private sector methods can produce significant cost savings.

CONTRACTING OUT ANCILLARY SYSTEMS

The notion that the public educational sector has eschewed market mechanisms is an interesting fiction. Many public school administrators believe that most noninstructional areas can be handled more efficiently by private firms.[29] Moreover, for decades, public school systems have contracted with private companies to provide a wide range of services and functions, such as food, transportation, textbooks, instructional materials and supplies, skills and psychological assessment, custodial care, building maintenance and repair, new construction, accounting and payroll, benefits and pension management, data processing and information management, telecommunications infrastructure, even legal representation.[30] To help restructure and downsize their central administrations, several urban districts, including New York City, Minneapolis, and Chicago, have sought the assistance of large national management consulting firms and corporate reengineering groups, sometimes *pro bono* and sometimes at cost.

But the history of public sector contracting out shows that the practice has a complicated balance sheet.[31] Many school systems have discovered themselves victims of fraud, overcharging, defective product delivery, and other forms of corruption. Just as research has demonstrated little sustained difference between appointed and elected school boards,[32] the ineptitude of public bureaucracies has often been balanced by the creative misrepresentations of private contractors. Therefore school systems have oscillated between public and private provision of critical functions, particularly transportation, building maintenance, and custodial care.[33]

In addition to using private sector services, public schools have attempted to increase their efficiency in other ways. Through decentralization reforms, power and authority are being shifted from states and districts to the local school level, and allocation and budgeting authority once monopolized by district administrations is increasingly being devolved to and shared with schools. As fiscal accountability moves to local schools, principals, teachers and parents are exercising more control over school budgets and costs. The object is to increase efficiency by giving those frontline personnel the right to make critical decisions about expenditure for instruction, curriculum, textbook selection, professional development, and school organization.

In Chicago, for example, a state legislative reform created locally elected school councils, equivalent to mini-school boards, for every

Chicago school. These councils, composed of parents, teachers, and community members but dominated by parents, approve the school's budget and have complete jurisdiction over the supplementary, state-supported compensatory education program, a funding stream that provides more than $500,000 annually for many Chicago schools. (The councils also hire and fire the principals, who work on four-year, renewable contracts rather than tenure.) These councils have enhanced instructional staffing and thereby reduced student/teacher ratios through their discretionary expenditures.[34]

In Kentucky, a statewide reform in 1989 created similar, locally elected councils with a different mix of parents and teachers. These councils receive discretionary funding from their local school board; they are also responsible for developing an annual school improvement plan and overseeing the expenditure of their school's budget to insure that the plan is effectively implemented.

As more funds are shifted to school-level use, school and district budgets are also becoming more transparent. The resulting fiscal accountability has begun to demonstrate a payoff in the more efficient use of education funds.[35]

INSTRUCTIONAL COSTS

Public education's more judicious critics recognize that many ancillary functions may be contracted out; but they see an unnecessary line drawn at instruction. Yet, for several decades districts have contracted out arts instruction by bringing specialists in dance, theater, film and video, and a variety of other art forms into classrooms.[36] Districts have collaborated with universities and their departments of education for student teachers, in-service professional development for teachers, and advanced training for district supervisory and administrative personnel.[37] Public school authorities have also provided funding through contracts or competitive grants to community-based organizations that offer recreation, counseling, homework help, and adult education after school, as well as dropout prevention, mentoring, and counseling programs during school hours.[38]

More recently, districts have contracted out instruction and professional development in preventive health, particularly in the fight against AIDS, sexually transmitted diseases, and substance abuse. They are also employing outside organizations to provide instruction to students and professional development for teachers in violence prevention and conflict resolution.[39] Finally, federal legislation granting educational rights to the handicapped has led to a series of lawsuits forcing school districts to contract with medical providers and private schools for services and instruction for students with disabilities. Approximately 7 percent of New York City's almost $8 billion public education budget goes to private special education schools, private preschools serving children with disabilities, and private providers of services to children with disabilities.[40]

Yet the use of private schooling for special education has generated a host of charges and countercharges, from legislators as well as practitioners in the teaching community, about unnecessarily isolated and expensive placements.[41] Since 1985, several states have radically revamped their special education funding and program organization to move students with disabilities into mainstream programs, in part to decrease segregation, in part to lower their costs, and in part because of their inability to hold private providers accountable.[42]

Thus, the charge that public education systems maintain inefficient monopolies oversimplifies a far more complex and continually shifting reality. Despite their mixed experiences, public school systems continually experiment with companies and nonprofit organizations to deliver many noninstructional services and even some instructional functions. Urban public schools are becoming more cost conscious, more data driven, and more accessible to the parents and citizens who are their primary constituents.

PARENTAL INVOLVEMENT: VOICE AND CHOICE

Although privatizers often attack American public education for being compulsory and allowing no parental choice, most urban systems have always offered some level of options. Many competitive and highly selective urban high schools have existed for more than fifty years, admitting students citywide on the basis of test results or previous academic performance. (Central High School in Philadelphia and Stuyvesant High School and Bronx High School of Science in New York are famous examples.)

The Supreme Court's first *Milliken* decision in 1972 eliminated two major strategies for desegregating increasingly nonwhite urban districts: cross-district busing and the consolidation of urban and surrounding suburban school districts. To increase pupil movement, local and federal desegregation policies turned to supporting magnet schools. Created as a way to enroll white students voluntarily in previously segregated inner-city schools, magnet schools have attempted to increase their racial and class mix by offering better facilities, a richer curriculum, lower teacher-student ratios, more instructional and support resources, and after-school programming.[43]

Several urban districts have used their magnet grants to develop extensive, districtwide choice programs. In Manhattan's District 4, choice now exists for all middle school students. Montclair, New Jersey; Cambridge, Massachusetts; and White Plains, New York, have instituted full-scale choice programs at both elementary and middle school levels. All four districts also have extensive parent information programs to encourage informed choice. Many other districts have developed magnets and other choice programs to increase the options available to students previously in zoned schools. However, in districts that retain some neighborhood schools, one of the persistent criticisms has been that choice programs select better-off and higher-performing students and thereby depress both motivation and achievement among students remaining in the zoned schools.[44]

In addition to expanding choice, several states and districts have initiated charter school programs in which a new or existing school is funded directly, controls its own budget, hiring, and curriculum, and is freed from most of the accountability requirements that weigh on local public schools. Charter legislation in some states imposes equity requirements on student selection procedures, while in other states it does not. In some states, charter legislation is also directed to freeing schools from collective bargaining. An ongoing debate about the implications of charters focuses on the fairness of their student recruitment processes and on their accountability to students, parents, and the taxpaying public.[45]

Finally, a few states have initiated cross-district choice programs through which students can enroll in any school in the state, regardless of location. While these programs do not pay student transportation costs, some reimburse the cost differentials between the sending and receiving districts. Experience thus far indicates minimal use of these programs, but insofar as families do take advantage of them, there is a pattern of student movement from resource-poor to privileged school districts that increases the fiscal burden on poor school districts forced to subsidize the higher costs of those students attending the more expensive districts.[46]

If privatizers have attacked public schools for lack of choice, others have accused them of limiting parental involvement to volunteerism and bake sales.[47] Yet here too there are significant changes. As the discussions above indicate, the decentralization of administration and governance is accompanied by increased involvement of parents in school-level decisions about budgets, hiring, curriculum, and school organization. Devolving power from district administrations to the school level means vesting discretionary authority in something resembling school-based councils comprising parents, teachers, and the school's administration. In Chicago alone, almost 15,000 parents and community members have been elected as local school council members since 1990.[48] National reform efforts such as Success for All, the School Development Program and Accelerated Schools have also increased parental participation.[49] Other programs have strengthened families' ability to support their children's overall development, readiness for schooling, and academic achievement.[50]

ACCOUNTABILITY

Until the latter half of this century, public education relied on two primary forms of accountability: fiscal and political. School systems were financially supported by a combination of state allocations and local tax bases, and this provided whatever fiscal accountability citizens and state legislatures deemed appropriate. District school boards composed of private citizens, elected or appointed, served as the locus of political accountability.[51]

FISCAL ACCOUNTABILITY

Fiscal accountability has been undergoing a dual shift, to more fiscal responsibility at the individual school level, and simultaneously to more state-level oversight and control. Budgets have become more transparent, and people running the local schools have become clearer about what funds are for and how they can be best used. But as states have increased their funding relative to district contributions, they have often increased their accountability requirements as well, mandating regular reporting on student demographics, district resource allocation, and student achievements.[52] Many state departments of education disseminate these findings as a public accountability measure. Other states monitor results, often in relation to a statewide set of standards, and require districts and schools to take corrective measures to improve poor performance. Some states base decisions to take over the administration of schools and districts on such measures.

For example, New Jersey passed legislation allowing its education department to take over districts judged educationally deficient; thus far, three urban districts—Jersey City, Paterson, and Newark—have been superseded. (Early evidence indicates improved fiscal and administrative procedures, but no improvements in academic achievement as evidenced by standardized test scores.[53]) New York State has recently done the same with the Roosevelt (Long Island) school district.

Standardized, multiple-choice testing, the most traditional form of assessing academic outcomes, has been the mainstay of state monitoring. But in response to growing nationwide critiques of such tests, several states have instituted varieties of more authentic, performance-based assessment such as portfolios, demonstrations, and longitudinal record keeping, as well as comprehensive external reviews of school practice.[54] These too are being incorporated into states' evaluations of both schools and districts.

BUREAUCRATIC ACCOUNTABILITY

When privatization advocates attack the failure of accountability in public education, their targets are often the compliance-driven urban bureaucracies that have evolved to monitor federal funds and to ensure students' rights and entitlements articulated by legislative and judicial mandates.[55] Since 1965, the federal government's provision of funding for compensatory, bilingual, and special education has created new procedural rules. Though Washington's allocations rarely amounted to more than 10 percent of any locality's education funding, federal accountability requirements have become quite complex. The necessary monitoring and oversight mechanisms have developed into bureaucracies that attempt to ensure observance of federal fiscal requirements (as well as of legislative and court mandates and the stipulations of union contracts).[56]

Federal court decisions in desegregation cases have also forced school systems to institute complicated student assignment methods and districtwide transportation arrangements. Special education legislation and court decisions have also led to complex systems of referral, evaluation, and placement, as well as new forms of instruction for students with disabilities.

In their complaints about the bureaucratic machinery of urban schools, privatization advocates ignore the judicial and negotiated rights, entitlements, and equity considerations that the machinery attempts to safeguard. The scale of bureaucracy in urban public school systems is often compared unfavorably with the minimal administration typical of Catholic school systems. Parochial schools are said to offer African-American and Latino students more integrated education without bureaucracy.[57] Yet this better record of integration results from the fact that, while public schools are attempting to ensure some level of desegregation in an educational system from which many white students have long fled, Catholic schools generally are not lacking for white students. Thus, students of color are simply more likely to be in classes with white peers.

Though the issue of how to guarantee that disadvantaged children receive an effective education has not been adequately resolved through unwieldy accountability procedures, privatization advocates have yet to demonstrate that market solutions will solve, or at least reduce, our current racial and ethnic inequalities.

Public systems have been moving to reduce bureaucratic and procedural accountability without ignoring or increasing the inequities these constraints were created to prevent. Reforms are decentralizing and downsizing central administrations and devolving some of their functions and responsibilities to local schools through school-based management and decisionmaking.[58] Some of these reforms have been mandated by state law, as in Kentucky; others have been negotiated through union contracts. In addition, many states have begun programs that grant waivers from procedural requirements to local schools in exchange for demonstrable results. How well these shifts will serve the cause of equity remains to be seen.

In some urban districts, political control is also moving from school boards to the mayor's office. Through changes in Illinois state law, for example, the Chicago school board has been effectively dissolved, and political control over public schooling has been vested in Chicago's mayor.[59] New York's mayor has been campaigning for similar authority, and several bills subjecting public education in New York City to mayoral control are pending in the state legislature.[60] Baltimore may well be experiencing a similar process.

In many large cities a permanent bureaucracy has evolved to handle grievance hearings, arbitration arrangements, and contractual rights negotiated by teachers unions.[61] However, these bureaucracies have become less pervasive in several urban districts as unions have begun to change their traditionally adversarial modes of operation. In Rochester, Toledo, Seattle, Cincinnati, and New York City, among others, unions are collaborating with district superintendents to improve the performance of ineffective teachers or counsel them out of the profession.

EQUITY

For the latter half of this century, American public education has been engaged in two critical efforts to promote equity: the desegregation of public schooling in response to the Supreme Court's 1954 decision in *Brown v. Board of Education* and the equalization of resources directed to schools, initiated through successive waves of lawsuits beginning with *Serrano v. Priest* in California in 1972 and *Robinson v Cahill* in New Jersey in 1975.[62]

DESEGREGATION

The implementation of equal access, particularly for students of color, has dominated the efforts of hundreds of school systems during the past four decades. Because states were often enjoined as defendants in these desegregation lawsuits, court decisions have forced states to allocate significant funding to pay for district reorganization.[63]

But the results of these desegregation efforts have been extremely limited and controversial. Although southern schools are currently far more integrated than they were fifty years ago, northern and midwestern schools, particularly in urban areas, are more segregated.[64] All of this has provoked a national debate not only about the utility of specific desegregation strategies but about the ultimate value of integration. Many educators and parents—both black and white—believe in the virtues of heterogeneous classrooms and schools.[65] But a number of African-American leaders have argued that ensuring an effective education for children of color is more important than diversity, and that national and local efforts should concentrate on providing the resources necessary for effective schooling even in settings of racial isolation.[66]

EQUALIZATION IN FUNDING

Past efforts at performance contracting and vouchers, as well as privatization efforts in Baltimore, Milwaukee, and Chelsea, indicate that privatizers have found it far easier to attack the equity shortcomings of public systems than to mitigate inequities through their own efforts.

Since the 1960s, lawsuits demanding equity in education funding have forced several states to increase spending and alter the pattern of their allocations.[67] The recent surge of second-generation equity lawsuits argues that state allocations for education are not only inequitable and discriminatory toward poor students and students of color, but also inadequate, in tax-poor districts, to reach state-defined standards of achievement. Suits based on these grounds have been successful in Kentucky and Alabama and are pending in New York.[68]

Yet every move toward fiscal realignment creates a political counteraction. Shifts of power to suburban constituencies in many state legislatures do not bode well for legislative decisions in favor of broad-based funding equity. This demographic change may well sustain the funding disparities that condemn urban school systems to subsistence on skeletal resources.[69]

Nevertheless, these tax equalization cases and the backlashes against them have forced extended debates about the responsibilities of states, municipalities, and taxpayers to ensure that all public school students have access to an adequate education. If some of these battles have paralyzed legislatures and contributed to the defeat of governors, that is often the cost of using democratic process to resolve critical questions about collective needs.

While privatizers have avoided these battles by accepting current inequities, and promising to create schools that will suit different "market niches," some of their supporters have claimed that money has no relationship to good schooling.[70] Yet if consumer preferences can be said to lead some shoppers to Sears, while others prefer Saks Fifth Avenue, our nation cannot afford to educate its future students in schools with similar disparities in quality and wealth. Avoiding questions of how to finance education in communities in desperate fiscal situations can only exacerbate our two-tiered system of schooling.

SCHOOLS AS A CIVIC SPHERE

Privatization threatens another critically important public purpose: the preparation of students for responsible citizenship. Traditionally, public schools have been expected to develop our collective capacity for effective participation in society by bringing together students from different racial, ethnic, and socioeconomic backgrounds in a common experience. The school reformer Deborah Meier makes this argument with characteristic passion:

> In school kids sit down next to their classmates, whoever they are. Parents proudly come together at school concerts, weep together at graduations, and congregate in times of crisis at public hearings and PTA meetings. Public schools therefore offer opportunity for a sense of community otherwise sorely missing, for putting faces and names to people we might otherwise see as mere statistics or categories.[71]

Meier demonstrates how public schools train students for "political conversation across divisions of race, religion, and ideology," pointing out that "in the clash of irreconcilable ideas" students learn how to test or revise ideas, or invent new ones.[72]

Detractors will argue that this vision of creativity through diversity is more myth than reality. Many city school systems, from which so many native-born white families have long since fled, serve almost entirely children of color. Moreover, by 2033 the majority of students American schools will be educating will be nonwhite.[73] Yet a closer examination of urban schools reveals a variety of ethnicities and cultures: from Central and South America and the Caribbean; from the Indian subcontinent; from China, Southeast Asia, and the Philippines; as well as from the countries of Eastern Europe and the former Soviet Union. The educational needs of this rich potpourri of immigrant and native-born students are no less urgent because few white students share their classrooms. If the future of our nation, and in particular the future of city dwellers, is dependent on the capacity for citizenship among this new multitude, what role must our schools play in assuring that student diversity becomes a source of cultural richness and strength?

Schools and school systems have begun to answer that question through varied forms of public examination, discussion and debate. In response to privatizers' criticisms of democracies' imperfect public mechanisms, one might well paraphrase Winston Churchill: Democracy is the worst form of government, except for all those other forms that have been tried over the years.[74] Moreover, their suggested alternative is divisive, for their "market niche" solution will bring together only people with like tastes and incomes.

Beyond providing students with respect and understanding for the diversity of the American experience, public schools have traditionally been expected to teach the basics of citizenship: this nation's history, literature, culture, and forms of governance. As we continually reinterpret our complex national heritage, what our students are taught about these subjects constantly changes. How should the topics that concern nation building be taught? What contexts should shape their presentation and analysis? And, most important, who should decide? All these questions are part of the current public debate.

Across the country, for example, there have been fierce controversies about how the exploration and colonization of North and South America should be depicted, as symbolized by the argument about how best to observe Columbus Day.[75] An even more contentious debate involves how schools should explore the role of Europeans, North Americans, and Africans in the centuries of trade in human beings that resulted in the system of slavery.[76]

In both industrialized and developing nations, critical decisions about the civics curriculum are often made by ministries of education ultimately responsible to national legislatures or parliaments. But because our Constitution defines education primarily as a state concern, such decisions here must be made at state and district levels through a public process of debate and discussion. Shaping our heritage so that the next generation can assimilate it as a guide to their era is a task too complex and too important to be left to providers operating outside our most critical public sphere.

7.

THE LIMITS OF PRIVATIZATION AND THE CONTINUING STRUGGLE FOR EQUITY

This scenario of a two-tier education system in the year 2010—one tier for the haves and another for the have-nots—is ugly. It's a scenario that would further stratify our . . . society . . . and undermine America's ability to produce an educated citizenry capable of meeting the challenges of the twenty-first century.

Don Cameron, "Preserving the American Dream"[1]

In the midst of the largest wave of immigration since the late nineteenth century, and a globalization of labor that has taken millions of U.S. jobs to other countries, a gnawing distress about American society's social and economic ills has often translated into dissatisfaction with public education. The restructuring of labor that has reduced our nation's middle class and deepened the divisions between rich and poor has also raised the levels of skill necessary for higher-wage jobs. Whether or not American students are performing below those in other countries, students in our cities, our suburbs, and our rural areas will need higher skills and more knowledge to have a chance at securing good jobs in the twenty-first century. The nostalgic lens through which older Americans view their education may be shaped less by the superiority of yesteryear's public schooling than by the far simpler tasks and demands public education confronted in the past.

The common perception of a failed public school system is really focused on urban districts, and it is buttressed daily by images of run-down school buildings, exposures of chronic fiscal shortfalls, and even instances of bankruptcy. Three decades of lawsuits in the name of fairness have done little to reduce the advantages of property-rich districts, which can fund their public schools more amply at lower tax rates than property-poor districts. Not surprisingly, many privileged families oppose these lawsuits and their efforts at redistributing tax dollars to improve the education of "other people's children." Yet the widespread agreement that this nation must have an educated populace if it is to remain a prosperous and internationally competitive society has created an urgency—at least in rhetoric— to improve schools for all students.

Nevertheless, resistance both to paying higher taxes and to restructuring public education finance has convinced some that private solutions offer an attractive solution. The notion that government has too much power has also made some believe that if the money currently spent on public schools could be given directly to families to use for the school of their choice, public education would simply disappear—as would the problems it faces. Others argue that since public schools, like other government institutions, are inefficient and wasteful, letting private corporations run schools will quickly make them more productive and cheaper, without the pain of additional taxation and fiscal restructuring.

For many privatization advocates, it is public school *systems* that are incapable of significant reform. Because they are mired in bureaucracy, with unions and other entrenched constituents locked into immobility, improvements will always be marginal, leaving most schools deeply troubled. The only solution, according to this view, is not just contracting out a single school but systematic overhaul. Private industry, with its expertise in operating at lower costs, is proposed as the ideal vehicle for this transformation. The corporate world's relentless focus on the bottom line, increased productivity, and efficiency through streamlining can make urban schools perform without threatening the current funding arrangement that allows affluent communities to ensure their children's futures by spending more on public education.

Although this report has focused on the privatization of public schooling in the United States, changes in the public/private balance are occurring within the context of a worldwide reconsideration of the relative roles of public and private sectors. This reconsideration has been most dramatic in Central and Eastern Europe and the former Soviet Union. But western European countries and Great Britain are also debating the appropriate size and responsibilities of government, and privatization is being considered as a policy option for many sectors including health, housing, and welfare. While discussions of school privatization have not been a top priority in Europe and the countries of the former Soviet

Union, African and Latin American nations have been experimenting with privatizing schools, generally with negative results in terms of both performance and equity.[2]

In the United States, dramatic changes in technology and the advent of a global corporate economy have altered labor-management relations and generated pressure on workers to give up what amounts to decades of gains in wages, insurance, and pensions. The movement to privatize American public schools goes hand in hand with this more general attack on unions. Because education is a labor-intensive sector, many privatizers see unions as the major obstacle to their promises to lower the costs of schooling. Conversely, school unions view privatizers as working to erode their membership and reverse their hard-won progress. As examples, they cite what has happened to public schools' support service personnel: from cafeteria workers and janitorial personnel to busing and security staffs, privatizers have circumvented the higher wages and better working conditions negotiated through collective bargaining. This antagonism played itself out in both Baltimore and Hartford, where the teachers' unions were a key force opposing privatization, and Education Alternatives, Inc., saw the unions as their major roadblock.

Finally, belief in the possibilities of privatization has been fueled by increasing disillusionment with government and democratic processes. Polls indicate that much of the public is cynical about the integrity of elected officials, including school board members. The rules and regulations by which government seeks to ensure equity and justice are increasingly seen as encroachments on individual freedom and liberty, and the compromises necessary to any democracy are often perceived as ineffective, even futile. For supporters of privatization, government and its vehicles are invariably intrusive, inefficient, and inadequate compared to the market, which always maximizes productivity and freedom.

THE RESULTS OF PAST EXPERIMENTS IN PRIVATIZATION

These arguments for privatization are not new. At the end of the Vietnam War, when the federal budget was attacked as bloated and public bureaucracies were perceived as autocratic and unwieldy, the federal government itself sponsored two major experiments in privatization. With federal support, a several-year voucher program was initiated in Alum Rock, California, in 1971. Directed at giving largely low-income Latino and African-American families greater choice in schools, the program began with six schools, each of which contained minischools. However, most families remained more eager to ensure that their children could continue in their neighborhood schools than to choose a new school, and participation reached its zenith of 18 percent in the third year. Some privatization advocates have argued that the voucher experiment in Alum Rock is not applicable to current privatization initiatives since it included only public schools. Certainly the fact that all the participating schools were public eliminated the risk of sudden school closings, as have occurred in Milwaukee's ongoing voucher program. Although cost was not an issue, since the Alum Rock district received federal funds to run the program, administering vouchers clearly added to the cost of schooling. Finally, although participating parents were positive about the program, vouchers in Alum Rock did not help raise the achievement levels of students.

In another early privatization experiment, between 1969 and 1972 more than two hundred school districts used performance contracting with private firms to deliver remedial reading and math and other basic skills to their low-income students, primarily students of color. While several of those districts received federal support, most were state-and locally supported programs. In Gary, Indiana, the school district went beyond contracting out for math and reading instruction, and paid a company to take over the running of an entire school. However, in none of the sites did performance contracting meet its promises to improve students' test scores—in some cases, its students did less well than corresponding groups of control students. Nor did performance contracting lower costs to the schools (or, in some cases, the federal government). Perhaps the strongest effect of performance contracting was to provoke in private firms a wariness about involvement in public education that lasted for more than twenty years.

Past privatization experiments also provide some lessons in accountability. Performance contracting sought to improve student outcomes by creating direct accountability by private contractors to the districts: firms would be paid according to the improved performance they generated. With the Alum Rock voucher experiment, by contrast, the locus of accountability was parents, who by choosing the schools their children attended would be empowered to shape the education options available to them.

However, both experiments failed to generate advances even in the limited areas of accountability they sought to develop. While performance contracting removed control over schooling from teachers, school administrators, and parents, the addition of private companies encumbered schools and districts with a new level of bureaucracy. In Alum Rock, despite the money spent on informing parents, by the end of the experiment only a bare majority of all families understood that they could transfer their children to another school and that transportation was free;

moreover, very few families had any knowledge of the curriculum and instructional variations that the district's schools offered their children.

In the past several years, as privatization has once again been proffered as a solution to public education's inadequacies, school districts have begun to experiment with contracting out schools to nonprofit and for-profit organizations, and offering families vouchers to be used in private, non-sectarian schools. The stories of these experiments have been told in detail here. Boston University is halfway through its ten-year takeover of the Chelsea school district, and it now claims that "survival" has been its real success.[3] Beyond survival, however, the takeover's effects on the Chelsea schools have been complicated and the reviews mixed: there have been important additions to the school districts' offerings, like early childhood education and music classes. But there has been no apparent improvement in students' academic performance, and the project continues to offer limited scope for parent participation. Friction also continues between the university and the school district.

The Milwaukee experiment with vouchers for low-income students is in its fifth year; although participating parents are satisfied with the program, the record of attrition complicates the picture. While initial studies showed no achievement gains for children in choice schools, a more recent re-analysis claims some improvement. In both Baltimore and Hartford, Education Alternatives has lost its contracts, in the former instance after three and a half years, and in the latter after just eighteen months. Finally, after much initial fanfare and extravagant promises in the late 1980s, the Chicago Corporate Community School's effort to develop a model for how business can improve schooling was abandoned after four years, and the school was taken over by the Chicago public system.

As with performance contracting in the 1970s, privatization initiatives in the 1990s have been trumpeted as solutions for the difficulties in learning encountered by low-income students and students of color. The schools and districts experimenting with privatization are largely urban, and they have been struggling with severely depleted budgets. Even in Hartford, a city that has had relatively high per-pupil spending, endemic budget problems drove the district to seek private management. Suburban and other property-rich public school districts serving affluent, predominantly white students are not seeking to privatize; their families are generally satisfied with the public education their children receive. For many of these suburban districts, even "school choice" is seen as unnecessary and unattractive—merely a way of bringing urban children into their schools.[4] Clearly, all schools should be worth choosing, yet it is urban students in poor districts who too often are given the "privilege" of choosing among schools not as well supported and equipped as their counterparts in the suburbs, and who are the subjects of privatization experiments.

In a number of states, recent charter legislation has explicitly focused on schools serving disadvantaged students, not because these students need better schools (which they certainly do), but because politicians understand that middle-class families are generally satisfied with their well-funded public schools and would resist firms seeking to extract a profit from their children's education.[5]

The results of the privatization experiments previously described are summarized below using the five analytic lenses employed throughout this report.

OUTCOMES

Privatizers' overarching promise has been that privatization will lead to school improvement, narrowly defined as increased student achievement on standardized tests. Yet current experiments offer little support for even this restricted claim. In Baltimore, where the effort has been most thoroughly studied, there is no evidence for significant gains in student test scores under privatization, or for substantial differences between students in privatized and public schools. While there may be merit to the argument that too little time has elapsed for change to take effect, this was not the premise of the privatizers. As EAI's John Golle proclaimed at the onset of his venture in Baltimore, "In a sentence, we either dramatically improve student performance WITHOUT spending more money or our contract is cancelled."[6]

According to market theory, tying schools to consumer preference ensures improvement by eliminating those schools that do not succeed. However, results from the Milwaukee voucher program, as well as studies of a variety of public school choice programs, make clear that "greater choice is unlikely, *by itself*, to enhance the performance of schools [italics in original]."[7] When school choice does enhance student performance, it is because it has been coupled with strong educational reform measures.

These privatization experiments also suggest that an unrestrained market can pose serious problems for students. Twice in the course of the Milwaukee experiment, students were suddenly stranded in midyear when their schools closed as a result of fiscal problems. Schools differ substantially from shoe stores or restaurants that disappear from one day to the next for lack of business, and students are not merely consumers. If privatization sets in motion a Darwinian world in which only the fittest schools survive, some protections must be secured for students enrolled in schools that go under.

The privatization movement emerged during a period when criticisms of traditional achievement tests were generating alternate ways to measure learning in public school systems throughout the country. Portfolios and what practitioners call authentic assessment were being created by public school teachers at all levels, and several state departments of education were incorporating these new methods into their testing programs. Unfortunately, none of the privatization experiments have participated in this movement; instead, the contracts between privatizers and schools or districts—including the one between Boston University and Chelsea—were conditioned on very narrow educational outcomes as measured by standardized tests.

Nor are agreements between school districts and privatizers likely to lead to innovations in assessment methods. Both sides want clear-cut, easily understandable—which means already well-known—ways of describing and measuring student achievement. Moreover, since privatizers are under strong pressure to lower costs, they are unlikely to incorporate testing programs that are labor-intensive, even when, as in Baltimore, traditional testing restricts the breadth of the curriculum they themselves offer. Thus, insofar as privatization efforts expand, experiments in enriching assessment and diversifying curriculum are likely to be stymied.

The story of Education Alternatives in Baltimore makes clear exactly how standardized testing can undermine innovation. EAI advertised a lively curriculum as part of its Tesseract program. But though this curriculum seemed to complement new forms of assessment, EAI's contract with the Baltimore City Public Schools forced students in the Tesseract schools to be assessed by traditional multiple-choice tests. Pressure to meet EAI's contractual agreement for test score improvement then worked against teachers using the more imaginative Tesseract curriculum. As the University of Maryland evaluation pointed out, by the third year, the Tesseract schools were instructionally indistinguishable from other public schools in the city, except in that Tesseract students were spending more time in test preparation and being tested.[8]

The problems with privatizers' focus on standardized testing are larger and more serious than the narrowing scope of learning imposed by a test-driven curriculum. Students' cognitive gains are just one of the goals of schooling. If our country is to maintain a healthy economy and fulfill its democratic potential, it needs much more from schools than those basic skills measurable by standardized tests. The larger vision of an American educational system, which includes helping to ensure students' physical and mental health and maximizing their opportunity to become productive citizens who participate in civic life, is likely to shrivel under privatization.

COST

In a period of deepening fiscal crises, one of the critical attractions of privatization has been its promise to cut costs. "Better government at half the price! Private production of public services"[9] might well be the general motto. Yet in the Tesseract schools in Baltimore, the average cost per pupil was 11.2 percent higher than in the other Baltimore City Public Schools. While the Chicago Corporate Community School was developed to show that business could run a successful school for the same per-pupil costs as the Chicago public schools, its corporate directors soon realized the necessity for supplementing their school's budget.

By contrast, Boston University has made no pretense of living within the Chelsea school district's starvation budget. One of the university's first acts after signing the partnership agreement was to create a foundation whose sole purpose was to solicit extra funds. Although the Milwaukee voucher program has cost the city less per pupil than the average for students attending the Milwaukee Public Schools, there are no data on how much it has actually cost the participating schools to educate the voucher-bearing students. The succession of school closings suggests that the vouchers supplied to students may not meet their schooling costs.

In both Hartford and Baltimore, the contract with Educational Alternatives was rescinded by the school districts, in large part because the company refused to renegotiate payment or resource allocation when the districts encountered tax shortfalls. Since tax revenues change each year, public sector services in general, and public education in particular, have always factored in painful budgetary bargaining as part of their operating mode. If private companies demand that their contracted fees be honored, no matter what fiscal constraints schools face, school districts may well be forced into even deeper financial difficulties.

Yet EAI and other private firms hope to make a profit from working in precisely those urban districts suffering from chronic shortfalls. Their strategy focuses on cutting personnel costs by reducing teacher numbers through heavier reliance on the one-time expense of computers for instruction and by using nonunion workers. Until now, the teachers' unions have succeeded in protecting teachers and other professional staff. Thus, cost trimming by privatizers has focused on classroom paraprofessionals, bus drivers, cafeteria workers, and janitorial staff. Since these workers often come from the same communities as the students, the economic benefits of reducing their numbers must be balanced against the denial of these jobs to localities that already have high levels of unemployment, as well as the loss of neighborhood representatives in the schools.

Although good teachers present a central expense in education budgets, teachers' salaries lag behind those of other college-educated professionals. In recent decades, the quality of teachers has decreased as talented individuals who might once have entered the field have chosen more lucrative professions. Thus, insofar as privatizers are able to lower pay scales, it is likely that teaching will become still less competitive and teacher quality further reduced. Moreover, although the use of computers to replace teachers may well be financially advantageous, this is a questionable instructional strategy, particularly in neighborhoods where children often lack sustained and supportive contact with adults.

Recent privatization experiments have focused solely on per-pupil costs—a ratio of resources to students—to make their efficiency claims. Since schools aim to educate, costs would more rationally be calculated as a relationship between resources and student success. Though it may be difficult to judge whether a school has produced well-educated and responsible citizens, proxy indicators such as attendance, credits achieved, graduation rates, college acceptances, and other, more diverse and authentic results could be used to suggest the extent and quality of school performance. One possible formula might be a ratio of resources to how much a student has progressed towards an educational objective over a specified period of time, a measure of the value each school contributes to a student's knowledge, skills, and capacities.[10] The performance contracts of the 1970s, by tying payment to students' progress, offered a simple version of this formula. Today, Public Strategies, Inc., the private firm that has taken over the Minneapolis school system, is charging a base rate with bonuses tied to improvements in several areas, including students' test scores. However, companies like EAI have been unwilling to go beyond promises and actually link their rewards to how much progress students make in their schools.

Finally, a primary concern for companies like EAI, which are listed on the stock market, must be to show a healthy financial picture to investors. News of improved test scores in EAI's Baltimore schools (falsely reported, as it turned out) caused stock prices to shoot up. In Hartford, funds received from the district were reported as profits in order to drive up interest in the company's stock. Although EAI has announced that it will back away from contracts with urban districts, education is touted as a new growth industry. Publicly traded education companies' stocks rose more than 32 percent between April 1995 and April 1996, compared with 13 percent for the NASDAQ composite index.[11] Beyond the issue of whether public schooling will prove to be the cash cow depicted by investment companies, the correlation between high stock prices and a rich education for our nation's children remains weak.

PARENTAL INVOLVEMENT

Because the research showing that parents' involvement enhances student success is so clear, most of the current privatization experiments have had a parental component. Although the Chelsea-Boston University partnership did not include choice for families, establishing links between parents and schools was a key part of the university's commitments to the Chelsea district. Boston University has presented a variety of opportunities for parents to improve their academic and parenting skills but has rarely solicited family opinions on or involvement in schooling decisions. Thus, Chelsea parents have been limited to predominantly passive roles, periodically voicing anger at the university's autocratic management style.

Similarly, in Baltimore, EAI did not offer a choice of schools or programs, although families and teachers could choose to withdraw from EAI schools. While the Tesseract program included several packaged formats to bring families into the school to talk with teachers, parents did not appear more involved in the Tesseract schools than in other BCPS schools.

Parents participating in Milwaukee's voucher program already had a high level of involvement in their children's education, as measured by their reports of contacts with their previous schools and of helping with homework and reading to their children. Indeed, the Milwaukee experiment adds weight to the finding of other research that choice programs attract the more involved parents. If choosing a school represents a further act of involvement, then the Milwaukee voucher program also increased parental engagement for these families. However, the one-time exercise of choice could have taken place within a public choice system; it is not inherently restricted to privatization.

Creating genuine parent involvement that goes beyond choice, or bake sales and other forms of volunteerism, has proved extremely difficult for schools. Nevertheless, a number of urban public school systems have succeeded in involving families in significant school-level decisions about budgets, hiring, curriculum, and school organization. These efforts stress parental voice rather than choice; they give parents genuine decisionmaking power in school affairs. Because privatizers tend to define parent involvement primarily as an act of consumerism, privatized schools are likely to remain outside those developments that give families a genuine voice in schooling.

ACCOUNTABILITY

As with the experiments in the 1970s, privatization in the 1990s has focused on different aspects of accountability, but its success has at best been mixed. One strong current in the privatization movement has been to contract out the running of schools to private nonprofit or for-profit companies. The focus, as in performance contracting, has been on accountability between the company and the school district, with families left out of the loop.

Yet in actual practice, current contracting out efforts have been quite spongy with respect to accountability. While city and school district officials in both Baltimore and Hartford were sufficiently displeased with Education Alternatives to cancel their deals, in both instances the contracts with the firm were hastily drawn and notably vague, leaving EAI a good deal of latitude to make a variety of organizational and staffing changes without seeking approval. In Baltimore, the company proceeded unilaterally to repair buildings, install computers—all to the good—as well as to alter staffing, a more controversial intervention. Moreover, the reporting of test scores, as well as the comparisons drawn with other public schools in the city, became a prime source of conflict. In both Baltimore and Hartford, the company's unwillingness to consider its accountability to the districts was evident when tax shortfalls forced a districtwide reallocation of funding.

While public institutions can be wracked by fiscal scandals and disagreements over taxation policies and funding priorities, the law allows both nonprofit organizations and for-profit companies greater shielding from public scrutiny. Open meeting laws and freedom of information are also foreign to the corporate culture. When the Government Accounting Office attempted an analysis that would compare spending in Baltimore's public and privatized schools, EAI denied access to its records. Nor has Boston University, a private institution, been eager to yield privacy: there has been constant discord because the university insists on less public disclosure and discussion than Chelsea constituencies have demanded.

The Chicago Corporate Community School was initiated to demonstrate the superiority of corporate-run education. But once the fervor of early promotion was over, the directors provided no information about either students' achievement or the prospects of the school, presumably because it experienced considerable difficulties in its operations.

There may well be merit to the corporate saying, "You give us the power, we'll do the job." However, schools have traditionally been an important focus for public debate about community priorities, and American families rightfully believe that they should be able to influence

what and how their children learn. Although too often government institutions lack integrity and betray the public trust, business world chicanery
and illegality are frequent enough to suggest that embracing corporations
is a questionable way to achieve greater accountability.

Voucher experiments offer a very different picture of what is gained
and lost with respect to accountability. Although parents in Milwaukee
were more satisfied with the private schools they had chosen than with
their former public schools, this satisfaction may be linked more to the
opportunity for choice itself than to privatization. Moreover, parents
remained largely unaware of the purposes, specializations, or variation in
instructional methods within the schools they chose. As important, neither parents nor the Milwaukee school system had up-to-date information about the financial conditions of participating private schools; thus,
there was no protection for families and students when participating private schools failed.

Voucher partisans criticize public school systems as overly regulated
and have demanded that vouchers be accompanied by minimal or no government regulation. Yet the Milwaukee experience makes clear that a
voucher system can become chaotic, putting students at risk as schools
open and close. Nor is the problem of basing accountability on market
mechanisms limited to schooling. In the managed care field, where private firms were permitted to sign up Medicaid enrollees, companies seized
the opportunity to generate new profits without providing adequate services. State and federal governments were forced to intervene and stop the
enrollment process, and when the program begins again there is likely to be
stiffer regulation. Given a long history of similar experiences in other fields,
it is unlikely that a public school voucher system, once enacted, would be
unaccompanied by regulatory controls. Instead, as some conservatives have
feared, vouchers might well generate an expansion of the power of state
departments of education, as states produced new regulations to protect
families and their children from abuses by private institutions.[12]

EQUITY

Advocates of privatization have addressed equity issues in several
ways. Some argue that privatization will improve the education of children
poorly served by underfunded public schools. This position becomes most
explicit in the case of vouchers and other choice programs, which are
often touted as offering low-income children and families the same freedom to select good schools that has always been available to middle-class
and affluent students. Like the Alum Rock voucher program in the 1970s,
the Milwaukee voucher system has directly targeted low-income students.

Yet privatizers such as Education Alternatives have entered urban districts whose budgets are already far lower than those of the surrounding, property-rich suburban districts in the hope of extracting profits. Beyond whatever waste these companies succeed in trimming from the system, the pressure to cut costs has already affected equity in several ways. In Milwaukee, private schools joining the voucher program were exempted from the costly rules governing the education of disabled students in public schools. In Baltimore, EAI economized by taking special education students out of separate classes with low teacher-student ratios and placing them with other students in much more crowded classes. Though many educators believe in mainstreaming, federal law stipulates that mainstreamed students must continue to receive their Individualized Education Plans. In Baltimore, special education students did not receive those plans, nor was their progress after mainstreaming evaluated to ensure that they were not harmed by the reduction of instructional attention.

The privatization experiments outlined here have been entirely isolated from the major equity-related struggles taking place within public education, detached from attempts at racial desegregation and from the battles to offer all students equally funded public schools. If privatization becomes a strategy to maintain the funding inequities that protect privileged communities and restrict lower-income students of color to an inferior education, then the divisions between rich and poor in this country, and the attendant social problems, will only increase.

WHAT MAY BE LOST THROUGH PRIVATIZATION

Despite the enthusiasm of its advocates, privatization has not proved itself a solution to low student achievement or declining school budgets. Moreover, it has not improved accountability, widened parents' involvement, or increased equity. The cancellations of EAI's contracts in Baltimore and Hartford, the brief life of the Chicago Corporate Community School, and the limitations of the other initiatives suggest that privatization is not the panacea its advocates claim. Its problems seem to outweigh its prospects.

There are several vital areas in which students and the nation at large are likely to lose should more schools and districts attempt to solve their problems through privatization. Most important, severe criticisms have helped to generate a wide variety of innovations throughout our public school systems. Despite the myth of public education's intractability, the past decade has seen lively experimentation. Districts have introduced school choice, with magnet schools, alternative schools, and Beacon schools providing health and social services alongside education. Significant strides have also been made in the development of curriculum and assessment techniques, and authority has been devolved considerably within districts and even within individual schools. All this would come to a halt if public schools were increasingly turned over to the private sector.

Public discussion and decisionmaking, however cantankerous and cumbersome, has been a key strength of public schools. Debates about curriculum, tracking, teacher preparation and development, as well as about how to educate students with special needs, have traditionally been conducted in environments that foster differences of opinion and tolerate conflict. Such frankness rarely characterizes corporate culture; instead, businesses habitually shield themselves from open discussion and public criticism. Yet it is through such processes of public discussion and decisionmaking that agendas come to reflect a popular will and that democracy is ultimately made to work.

While privatization has been driven in part by the desperation of underfunded urban public schools, the urgency to solve the inequities in schooling is perhaps the most important reason for continuing the struggle to reform *public* education. For we will not survive as a republic nor move toward a genuine democracy unless we can narrow the gap between rich and poor, reduce our racial and ethnic divides, and create a deeper sense of common purpose.

More than forty years after *Brown v. Board of Education*, while southern schools are generally less segregated, northern schools are more so. In spite of many effectively desegregated systems and schools, the extent of racial isolation in major U.S. cities is comparable to or worse than that of the era before the movement to integrate America. Moreover, in spite of three decades of struggles for fairness, disparities in funding between urban and suburban schools are increasing throughout the nation. It is almost as if, faced with the grand uniting vision of the *Brown* court, the nation has lost its nerve and opted for turning its back on the critical schooling needs of its least fortunate children.

The societal price we pay for such abandonment grows daily more painful: escalating turmoil and violence in our cities; a burgeoning underground economy trafficking in drugs, weapons, and other vice; a growing prison system imposing huge costs on the tax base; the ballooning price paid by business for entry-level training programs. Anyone wishing to see a dramatic demonstration of the country's polarization into two unequal societies need only visit a neighboring suburban and urban school system.

Whether or not the privatization movement continues to spread, it will remain marginal to the task of producing an effective education for *all* children. It may seem an act of nostalgic idealism in this difficult period to envision a national recommitment to provide effective schooling for poor children and students of color. Yet teachers, administrators, parents, elected officials, and policymakers struggle daily to respond effectively to their diverse students in classrooms and schools across the country. What supports the forces of cynicism and despair—and hence of privatization—are economic trends that tighten the screws on America's shrinking middle class. These pressures increase families' anxieties about the future and heighten parental efforts to secure schooling that gives their children an edge in a world that increasingly links high wages and high skills.

Between these two visions—of an America increasingly polarizing into armed camps of privilege and disadvantage or of a nation responding to the diversity of its citizens with a renewed commitment to offering all children an equal opportunity to learn—our public schools struggle to survive and to meet their students' needs. If privatization efforts are likely to remain irrelevant to those struggles, it is incumbent on those who believe in a strong public education system as a precondition for democracy to help resolve the grave inadequacies of public schooling that feed the impulse to privatize.

NOTES

1.

1. Pedro A. Noguera, "More Democracy Not Less: Confronting the Challenge of Privatization in Public Education," *Journal of Negro Education* 63, no. 2 (Spring 1994): 237.

2. Lawrence Ogle and Patricia Dabbs, "Good News, Bad News: Does Media Coverage of the Schools Promote Scattershot Remedies?" *Education Week*, March 13, 1996, p. 46.

3. Stanley M. Elam, Lowell C. Rose, and Alec M. Gallup, "The 26th Annual Phi Delta Kappan/Gallup Poll of the Public's Attitudes toward the Public Schools," *Phi Delta Kappan*, September 1994, pp. 42–56.

4. Jean Johnson and John Immerwahr, *First Things First: What Americans Expect from Public Schools* (New York: Public Agenda Foundation, 1994); Jean Johnson, *Assignment Incomplete: The Unfinished Business of Education Reform* (New York: Public Agenda Foundation; Washington, D.C.: Institute for Educational Leadership, 1995).

5. National Commission on Excellence in Education, *A Nation at Risk: The Imperative of Educational Reform* (Washington, D.C.: Government Printing Office, 1983), p. 5.

6. Kurt Schmoke, quoted in Joseph T. Viteritti, "Stacking the Deck for the Poor: The New Politics of School Choice," *Brookings Review*, Summer 1996, p. 12.

7. Elam, Rose, and Gallup, "26th Annual Phi Delta Kappan/Gallup Poll," p. 43.

8. Council of Great City Schools, "Diversifying Our Great City School Teachers: Twenty Year Trends," *Urban Indicator* 1, no. 1 (October 1993).

9. U.S. Congress, House, *Hearing on the Challenges Facing Urban and Rural Schools Before the Subcommittee on Elementary, Secondary, and Vocational Education of the Committee on Education and Labor*, 102nd Cong., 1st sess., November 14, 1991.

10. Robert D. Putnam, "Bowling Alone: Democracy in America at the End of the Twentieth Century," draft manuscript, Harvard University, August 1994.

11. Ibid.

12. Jeffrey Kane, "Choice: The Fundamentals Revisited," in Peter W. Cookson, Jr., ed., *The Choice Controversy* (Newbury Park, Calif.: Corwin Press, Inc., 1992), pp. 51, 59.

13. Milton Friedman, *Capitalism and Freedom* (Chicago: University of Chicago Press, 1962).

14. David W. Kirkpatrick, *Choice in Schooling: A Case for Tuition Vouchers* (Chicago: Loyola University Press, 1990).

15. Stephen Arons, *Compelling Belief* (New York: McGraw-Hill, 1983).

16. See John A. Gliedman, "The Choice between Educational Privatization and Parental Governance," *Journal of Law and Education* 20, no. 4 (1991): 395–419. Also see Paul Starr, "The Meaning of Privatization," *Yale Law and Policy Review* 6, no. 6 (1988): 6–41.

17. Starr, "Meaning of Privatization," p. 14.

18. Norm Fruchter et al., "Focus on Learning! A Report on Reorganizing General and Special Education in New York City," Institute for Education and Social Policy, New York University, 1995.

19. For a brief history of how this decision occurred, see Ira Krensky, "Getting Down to Business," *American School Board Journal*, April 1994, pp. 26–30.

20. GAO report, 1996.

21. See Diane Ravitch, "In Deep Denial," *New Democrat* 8, no. 1 (January/February 1996): 23.

22. This term is taken from the New American Schools Development Corporation.

23. Starr, "Meaning of Privatization," pp. 6–41.

24. James R. Rinehart and Jackson F. Lee, *American Education and the Dynamics of Choice* (New York: Praeger, 1991).

25. Jeffrey Henig, "The Danger of Market Rhetoric," in Robert Lowe and Barbara Minerm, *Selling Out Our Schools* (Milwaukee: Rethinking Schools Institute, 1996), p. 11; see also Jeffrey Henig, *Rethinking School Choice: Limits of the Marketplace Metaphor* (Princeton, N.J.: Princeton University Press, 1994).

26. Henig, "Danger of Market Rhetoric," p. 11.

27. Deborah A. Verstegen and Terry Whitney, "School Finance Litigation: Issues of Adequacy and Equity," paper prepared for a conference entitled "Thirty Years of Policy Analysis and Management: Taking Stock," American Public Policy and Management Association, Washington, D.C., November 3, 1995.

28. This argument is best articulated by John E. Chubb and Terry M. Moe, *Politics, Markets, and America's Schools* (Washington, D.C.: Brookings Institution, 1990).

2.

1. Denis P. Doyle, "The Role of Private Sector Management in Public Education, *Phi Delta Kappan*, October 1994, p. 129.

2. John McLaughlin, "The Private Management of Public Schools," *Principal* 73, no. 4 (March 1994): 19.

3. Mark Walsh, "Brokers Pitch Education as Hot Investment," *Education Week*, February 21, 1996, pp. 1, 15.

4. Chester E. Finn, "Why We Need Choice," in W. L. Boyd and H. J. Walberg, eds., *Choice in Education: Potential and Problems* (Berkeley, Calif.: McCutchan Publishing Corp., 1990).

5. Ben Brodinsky, "How 'New' will the 'New' Whittle American School Be?" *Phi Delta Kappan*, March 1993, p. 542.

6. John O'Leary and Janet R. Beales, "Education, Inc.," *Education Week*, December 15, 1993, pp. 13, 34ff.

7. Dick Armey, *The Freedom Revolution: The New Republican House Majority Leader Tells Why Big Government Failed, Why Freedom Works, and How We Will Rebuild America* (Washington: Regnery Publishing, 1995), p. 316.

8. Ernest L. Boyer, *School Choice: A Special Report* (Princeton, N.J.: Carnegie Foundation for the Advancement of Teaching, 1992), p. 50.

9. Amy S. Wells, *Time to Choose: America at the Crossroads of School Choice Policy* (New York: Hill and Wang, 1993).

10. Boyer, *School Choice*.

11. Mary E. Driscoll, "Choice, Achievement, and School Community," in Edith Rasell and Richard Rothstein, eds., *School Choice: Examining the Evidence* (Washington, D.C.: Economic Policy Institute, 1993), pp. 147–72. See also Boyer, *School Choice*.

12. Denis P. Doyle, "The Role of Private Sector Management in Public Education," p. 129.

13. Myron Lieberman, *Beyond Public Education* (New York: Praeger, 1986).

14. Paul Hill, *Reinventing Public Education* (Santa Monica, Calif.: RAND Corporation, 1995), p. x.

15. See, for example, Valerie E. Lee and Anthony S. Bryk, "Science or Policy Argument? A Review of the Quantitative Evidence in Chubb and Moe's *Politics, Markets, and America's Schools*," in Rasell and Rothstein, *School Choice*, pp. 185–208; the quote is from Ross Rubenstein, *Public and Private High School Differences: Findings from Four Important Studies* (New York: Institute for Education and Social Policy, March 1996).

16. John E. Chubb and Terry M. Moe, *Politics, Markets, and America's Schools* (Washington, D.C.: Brookings Institution, 1990), p. 217.

17. Ibid., p. 212.

18. Patsy Baker Blackshear, "The Tides of Change: Privatization in Education," *School Business Affairs* 59, no. 6 (June 1993): 30.

19. "An Interview with David Bennett, President, Educational Alternatives, Inc.," *School Business Affairs* 59, no. 11 (November 1993): 22–25.

20. Hill, *Reinventing Public Education*.

21. Claudia Wallis, "A Class of Their Own," *Time*, October 31, 1994, p. 57.

22. James R. Reinhard and Jackson F. Lee, Jr., *American Education: The Dynamics of Choice* (New York: Praeger, 1991).

23. Rolf K. Blank, "Analyzing Educational Effects of Magnet Schools Using Local District Data," *Sociological Practice Review* 1, no. 1 (1990): 40–51. See also

Paul T. Hill, Gail E. Foster, and Tamar Gendler, *High Schools with Character*, R-3944-RC (Santa Monica, Calif.: RAND Corporation, August 1990).

24. Brian L. Fife, *Desegregation in American Schools: Comparative Intervention Strategies* (New York: Praeger, 1992). See also Christine H. Rossell, "What Is Attractive about Magnet Schools?" *Urban Education* 20, no. 1 (April 1985): 7–22.

25. Debra Viadero, "Students Learn More in Magnets than Other Schools, Study Finds," *Education Week*, March 16, 1996, p. 6.

26. John M. McLaughlin, "The Private Management of Public Schools," *Principal* 73, no. 4 (March 1994): 17.

27. Hill, *Reinventing Public Education*, p. 50.

28. Lieberman, *Beyond Public Education*, p. 154.

29. Finn, "Why We Need Choice."

30. Lieberman, *Beyond Public Education*, p. 5.

31. David W. Kirkpatrick, *Choice in Schooling: A Case for Tuition Vouchers* (Chicago: Loyola University Press, 1990), p. 6.

32. Mark Walsh, "Brokers Pitch Education as Hot Investment," *Education Week*, February 21, 1996, p. 15.

33. Kirkpatrick, *Choice in Schooling*, p. 69.

34. Ibid., p. 53.

35. Cited in Brodinsky, "How 'New' Will the 'New' Whittle American School Be?" p. 542.

36. James T. Bennett and Manuel H. Johnson, *Better Government at Half the Price! Private Production of Public Services* (Aurora, Ill.: Caroline House Publishers, 1981).

37. Janet R. Beales, *Teacher, Inc.: A Private-Practice Option for Educators* (Los Angeles: Reason Foundation, October 1994).

38. Simon Hakim, Paul Seidenstat, and Gary W. Bowman, eds., *Privatizing Education and Educational Choice* (Westport, Conn.: Praeger, 1994), p. 9.

3.

1. Christopher Jencks, "Is the Public School Obsolete?" *The Public Interest*, Winter 1966, p. 21.

2. Leon Lesinger and Dwight. H. Allen, "Performance Proposals for Educational Funding: A New Approach to Federal Resource Allocation," *Phi Delta Kappan*, November 1969, p. 136.

3. Leon Lessinger, "Engineering Accountability for Results in Public Education," *Phi Delta Kappan*, December 1970, pp. 52, 217.

4. Telephone interview with Leon Lessinger, July 6, 1995; this and all subsequent interviews were conducted by Carol Ascher.

5. Three written sources were used in writing this story: Polly Carpenter, A. W. Chalfant, and George R. Hall, *Case Studies in Educational Performance Contracting: Texarkana, Arkansas; Liberty-Eylau, Texas*, prepared for the U.S.

Department of Health, Education and Welfare by the RAND Corporation, Santa Monica, Calif., December 1971; Ronald F. Campbell and James E. Lorion, *Performance Contracting in School Systems* (Columbus, Ohio: Charles E. Merrill Publishing Company, 1972), pp. 29–33; and George R. Hall et al., *The Evolution of Educational Performance Contracting in Five School Districts, 1971–72,* oration, (Santa Monica, Calif.: RAND Corp., 1972). In addition, telephone interviews were conducted with Leon Lessinger, former associate commissioner of education, as well as with Don Rader, former schoolteacher, and Grady Wallace, former principal, both in Texarkana public schools that had Rapid Learning Centers.

6. Telephone interview with Rader, July 6, 1995.

7. "Two Out of Three Boardmen Buy Performance Contracting," *American School Board Journal,* 1970, p. 35; cited in Campbell and Lorion, *Performance Contracting in School Systems,* p. 26.

8. Campbell and Lorion, *Performance Contracting in School Systems,* p. 10.

9. Donald M. Levine, ed., *Performance Contracting in Education—An Appraisal* (Englewood Cliffs, N.J.: Educational Technology Publications, 1972), p. 4.

10. Robert E. Stake, "Testing Hazards in Performance Contracting," *Phi Delta Kappan,* June 1971, p. 588.

11. The survey, conducted by Ronald F. Campbell and James E. Lorion, is cited in Campbell and Lorion, *Performance Contracting in School Systems,* p. 28.

12. Edward M. Gramlich and Patricia P. Koshel, *Performance Contracting* (Washington, D.C.: The Brookings Institution, 1975).

13. Stake, "Testing Hazards in Performance Contracting," p. 586.

14. Comptroller General of the United States, *Evaluation of the Office of Economic Opportunity's Performance Contracting Experiment,* report to Congress (Washington, D.C.: Government Accounting Office, 1973), p. 19.

15. Myron Lieberman, *Privatization and Educational Choice* (New York: St. Martin's Press, 1989), p. 100.

16. These three major research documents are: H. W. Ray, project director, *The Office of Economic Opportunity Experiment in Educational Performance Contracting* (Columbus, Ohio: Batelle Columbus Laboratories, March 1972); Comptroller General of the United States, *Evaluation of the Office of Economic Opportunity's Performance Contracting Experiment;* Hall et al., *Evolution of Educational Performance Contracting in Five School Districts* (in addition to this summary analysis, the RAND Corporation completed several case studies.

17. Comptroller General of the United States, *Evaluation of the Office of Economic Opportunity's Performance Contracting Experiment,* p. 80.

18. Gramlich and Koshel, *Performance Contracting,* p. 54.

19. George R. Hall and M. L. Rapp, *Case Studies in Performance Contracting: Gary, Indiana,* prepared for the U.S. Department of Health, Education and Welfare by the RAND Corporation, Santa Monica, Calif., November 1971. In addition, telephone interviews were conducted with Robert Hollyfield, former national sales director, Behavioral Research Laboratories; Allen Calvin, former chairman of the board, Behavioral

Research Laboratories; and Robert James, former elementary district administrator, Gary, Indiana.

20. Telephone interview with Hollyfield, July 7, 1995.

21. Hall and Rapp, *Case Studies in Performance Contracting.*

22. Ibid., p. 42.

23. Gramlich and Koshel, *Performance Contracting*, pp. 55–56.

24. Hall et al., *Evolution of Educational Performance Contracting in Five School Districts*, p. 37.

25. Carpenter, Chalfant, and Hall, *Case Studies in Educational Performance Contracting*, p. 41.

26. Donald Levine, "Major Problems in Performance Contracting for Education"; and Polly Carpenter, "An Evaluation of Performance Contracting for HEW," in Donald Levine, ed., *Performance Contracting in Education: An Appraisal* (Englewood Cliffs, N.J.: Educational Technology Publications, 1972), pp. 15, 23, and 36.

27. Campbell and Lorion, *Performance Contracting in School Systems*, p. 98.

28. Ibid., p. 99.

29. Ibid., p. 23.

30. Christopher Jencks, "Is The Public School Obsolete?" *Public Interest*, Winter 1966, pp. 23–24.

31. This story is drawn from David K. Cohen and Eleanor Farrar, "Power to Parents? The Story of Educational Vouchers," *Public Interest*, Summer 1977, pp. 72–97; and D. Weiler, *A Public School Voucher Demonstration: The First Year at Alum Rock*, prepared for the National Institute of Education by the RAND Corporation, Santa Monica, Calif., 1974.

32. Cohen and Farrar, "Power to Parents?" p. 84.

33. Ibid., p. 91.

4.

1. *Congressional Quarterly Researcher*, March 25, 1994, quoted in American Federation of Teachers, "The Private Management of Public Schools: An Analysis of the EAI Experience in Baltimore," AFT report, Washington, D.C., May 1994.

2. U.S. Government Accounting Office, *Private Management of Public Schools: Early Experiences in Four School Districts*, GAO/HEHS–96-3 (Washington, D.C.: Government Printing Office, April 1996), p. 1: 1.

3. Mark F. Goldberg, "Education in Baltimore," *Phi Delta Kappan*, November 1995, pp. 234–37.

4. Michael Winerip, "America Can," *Education Life*, November 9, 1993, pp. 15–18.

5. Kurt L. Schmoke was born in 1949 and grew up in Baltimore; his father had attended Morehouse College, and his mother Spelman College and Morgan State

University. In Baltimore he was enrolled in special college-prep programs that got him into Yale, followed by Oxford and Harvard Law School, graduating from the latter in 1976. He spent two years working in the administration of President Carter, then returned to Baltimore as assistant U.S. attorney in 1978. In the early 1980s he was elected state's attorney for Baltimore City, a position he held until elected mayor in November 1987. See Goldberg, "Education in Baltimore," pp. 234–37.

6. Winerip, "America Can," pp. 16–17.

7. Anne Wheelock, *The Baltimore City Institute for Middle School Reform: Mobilizing for District-Wide Middle Grades Innovation*, report prepared for the Edna McConnell Clark Foundation, Baltimore, June 1993, pp. 8–10.

8. The Abell Foundation, whose president, Robert C. Embry, Jr., is also chairman of the Maryland State Board of Education, ranks in asset size among the top 2 percent of the country's independent foundations. It has been an active supporter of such programs as Success for All. Its Barclay-Calvert Program, which allowed the Barclay School (where 82 percent of the students receive free lunch) to adopt the curriculum of the private Calvert School, showed major improvements in achievement and attendance after three years and is now the "template for achievement" in the Baltimore system. The Abell Foundation also funded the Dunbar Project, which formed alliances between schools, city agencies, and community groups. See Goldberg, "Education in Baltimore."

9. Wheelock, *Baltimore City Institute for Middle School Reform*, p. 15.

10. Joe Rigert, "Was EAI Start-up Financing Proper?" *Star Tribune* (Minneapolis), August 24, 1994, p. 1B.

11. Gary Patka and Steve Stecklow, "Fast Learner/Do For-Profit Schools Work? They Seem to for One Entrepreneur," *Wall Street Journal*, June 8, 1994, pp. A1, A4; American Federation of Teachers, *Education Alternatives, Inc.: What You Should Know*, AFT report, Washington, D.C., Fall 1992. See also American Federation of Teachers, "The Private Management of Public Schools," p. 3.

12. Peter Schmidt, "Private Enterprise," *Education Week*, May 25, 1994, pp. 27–30.

13. Thomas H. Peeler and Patricia A. Parham, "A Public-Private Partnership: South Pointe Elementary School of Dade County, Florida," in Simon Hakim, Paul Seidenstat, and Gary W. Bowman, eds., *Privatizing Education and Educational Choice: Concepts, Plans and Experiences* (Westport, Conn.: Praeger, 1994), pp. 195–204.

14. Ibid.

15. Tesseract, which comes from the famous children's book, *A Wrinkle in Time* by Madeleine L'Engle, is the trademark name for the instructional program used in all EAI schools.

16. "Schools that Work: Education Alternatives, Inc.," 1994 annual report, Education Alternatives, Inc., Minneapolis, p. 15; William Celis 3d, "Hopeful Start for Profit-making Schools," *New York Times*, October 6, 1993, pp. A1, B10.

17. Lois C. Williams and Lawrence E. Leak, *The UMBC Evaluation of the Tesseract Program in Baltimore City*, report, Center for Educational Research, University of Maryland, Baltimore County, September 1, 1995, p. 6.

18. American Federation of Teachers, "Private Management of Public Schools," p. 3.

19. Norman J. Walsh, "Public School, Inc.: Baltimore's Risky Enterprise," *Education and Urban Society* 27, no. 2 (February 1995): 196–97.

20. Stephen J. Ruffini, Lawrence F. Howe, and Denise G. Borders, "The Early Implementation of Tesseract: 1992–93 Evaluation Report," Department of Research and Evaluation, Baltimore City Public Schools, January 17, 1994, pp. 24–25; see also American Federation of Teachers, "Private Management of Public Schools," pp. 3, 5.

21. Ruffini, Howe, and Borders, "Early Implementation of Tesseract," pp. 20–24; Celis, "Hopeful Start for Profit-making Schools."

22. *Education Alternatives, Inc.*, p. 6; American Federation of Teachers, "Private Management of Public Schools," p. iii.

23. American Federation of Teachers, "Private Management of Public Schools," p. 16.

24. American Federation of Teachers, *EAI's Mismanagement of Federal Education Programs: The Special Education and Chapter 1 Track Records in Baltimore* (Washington, D.C.: AFT, December 1994).

25. Celis, "Hopeful Start for Profit-making Schools."

26. Ruffini, Howe, and Borders, "Early Implementation of Tesseract," pp. 6–7.

27. American Federation of Teachers, "Private Management of Public Schools," p. 2.

28. Ruffini, Howe, and Borders, "Early Implementation of Tesseract," pp. 45–46.

29. American Federation of Teachers, "Private Management of Public Schools," p. 2.

30. Peter Schmidt, "Baltimore's Amprey Backs Off Plan to Increase EAI Role," *Education Week*, June 22, 1994, p. 14; Gary Gately, "Council Members Seek Delay in EAI Expansion," *Baltimore Sun*, May 26, 1994, p. 1A.

31. American Federation of Teachers, "Private Management of Public Schools."

32. Joanna Richardson, "Private Firm Prompts Suit in Baltimore," *Education Week*, December 15, 1995, pp. 1, 13; quoted in Walsh, "Public School, Inc."

33. Gary Gately, "Amprey Won't Spend More to Expand EAI," *Baltimore Sun*, June 11, 1994, pp. 1A, 8A; news update, *Education Week*, June 15, 1994, p. 5.

34. American Federation of Teachers, *EAI's Mismanagement of Federal Education Programs.*

35. Ibid., p. 18.

36. Gary Gately, "Md. Cites 3 EAI Schools for Special Ed Violations," *Baltimore Sun*, July 8, 1994, pp. 1B, 2B.

37. Ibid.

38. Ibid.

39. American Federation of Teachers, *EAI's Mismanagement of Federal Education Programs*, p. xi; see also Ruffini, Howe, and Borders, "Early Implementation of Tesseract," p. 30.

40. American Federation of Teachers, "Private Management of Public Schools," p. 20.

41. Ibid.

42. Gary Gately and JoAnna Daemmrich, "Pressure Grows to Terminate EAI Experiment: Falling Test Scores in 'Tesseract' Schools Upset City Council," *Baltimore Sun*, October 19, 1994, pp. 1A, 12A.

43. Gary Gately, "Amprey Trips Paid for by EAI," *Baltimore Sun*, October 27, 1994, pp. 1B, 2B.

44. Gary Gately and JoAnna Daemmrich, "EAI Schools Fail to Match Citywide Attendance Gains," *Baltimore Sun*, October 29, 1994; "Stock Hurt by Article on Data," *Financial Report* (Reuters), October 18, 1994; William Celis 3d, "Group Admits School Gains Weren't Real," *New York Times*, June 7, 1994, p. A21.

45. Peter Schmidt, "Baltimore Mayor Seeks Changes in E.A.I. Contract," *Education Week*, March, 29, 1995, p. 3; see also Gately and Daemmrich, "Pressure Grows to Terminate EAI Experiment"; Gary Gately and JoAnna Daemmrich, "Mayor Links Future of EAI to Test Scores," *Baltimore Sun*, October 21, 1994, pp. 1B, 5B.

46. Jean Thompson and JoAnna Daemmrich, "Mayor Orders Changes in EAI Contract," *Baltimore Sun*, March 17, 1995, pp. 1A, 16A; Mayor Schmoke was under much pressure to make improvements in this election year, faced by a challenge for his third term by City Council president Mary Pat Clarke.

47. Gary Gately, "City Council to Check on EAI's Work," *Baltimore Sun*, December 8, 1994, p. 1A; Baltimore City Council, EAI Financial Oversight Committee, "Suggested Questions," April 3, 1995.

48. Mark Walsh, "Baltimore to Continue Contract with EAI to Run Nine Schools," *Education Week*, September 6, 1995, p. 14.

49. Williams and Leak, *UMBC Evaluation of the Tesseract Program*. In this section, this is referred to as the "evaluation report."

50. Ibid., p. 11.

51. Ibid., p. 11.

52. Ibid., p. 113.

53. Ibid., p. 5.

54. Ibid., p. 116.

55. Ibid., p. 4.

56. Ibid., p. 5.

57. Ibid., pp. 14–15.

58. Ibid., p. 16. Note that the evaluation report does not discuss the charges and reports reviewed in the first part of this chapter.

59. Ibid., p. 117.

60. Ibid., p. 34.

61. There is some variation in the per-pupil school-level costs of the comparison schools, ranging from a high of $5,845 to a low of $4,596. No information is provided on special education costs or the use of federal funding. See ibid., p. 34.

62. As noted in Williams and Leak, *UMBC Evaluation of the Tesseract Program*, p. 34, "The evaluation team has been looking for information on non-school

based costs for comparison schools and on central office-type functions carried out by EAI with school-based funds, but has not received any. Information provided by EAI repeated the assertion that EAI receives the school system average per-pupil costs, without addressing the issue of actual non-school based costs for the seven comparison schools."

63. Ibid., p. 115.

64. Ibid., p. 115.

65. Ibid., p. 48.

66. U. S. Government Accounting Office, *Private Management of Public Schools*, p. 2:1.

67. Williams and Leak, pp. 90–91. Tesseract schools obtained an average rating of 2.54 on the thirteen measured parent involvement activities, with a range of 1.92–3.17. This is slightly lower than the performance of the comparison schools, which obtained an average rating of 2.63, with a range of 1.23–3.38. Only one Tesseract school and one comparison school received a rating under 2.

68. Ibid., pp. 115–16, 118.

69. Ibid., pp. 116, 117.

70. Jean Thompson and Eric Siegel, "EAI Agrees to $7 Million Cut in Fees," *Baltimore Sun*, November 16, 1995, pp. 1B, 4B; Eric Siegel, "If EAI Takes Cut, It Wants Longer Deal," *Baltimore Sun*, November 19, 1995, pp. 1A, 22A.

71. Jean Thompson, "Parents Plan to Give Views on EAI Today," *Baltimore Sun*, November 20, 1995, pp. 1B, 2B; Jean Thompson, "Parents Press Schmoke on EAI," *Baltimore Sun*, November 21, 1995, pp. 1B, 4B.

72. Jean Thompson, "School Board Urges Mayor to Drop EAI," *Baltimore Sun*, November 22, 1995, pp. 1A, 11A; Jean Thompson, "Cutoff of EAI Saves Little," *Baltimore Sun*, November 23, 1995, pp. 1A, 19A.

73. Mark Walsh, "Baltimore to Terminate EAI Schools Contract," *Education Week*, November 29, 1995, pp. 1, 12.

74. Mark Walsh, "Baltimore Vote Ends City's Contract with EAI," *Education Week*, December 6, 1995, p. 6.

75. Ibid., p. 1.

76. Howard Libit, "School Test Scores Improve, but Only 40% 'Satisfactory,'" *Baltimore Sun*, December 13, 1995, pp. 1A, 10A.

5.

1. Steve Weiner, "We Decided to Show How Things Can Work," *Forbes*, September 18, 1989, p. 180.

2. Lisa Gubernick, "Midmarket Schools," *Forbes*, July 31, 1995, pp. 46–48.

3. Cited in Diane Pelavin, Peggy Siegel, and Rita Kirshstein, "Implementation of the Chelsea School Project: A Case Study," prepared for the Office of Planning, Budget, and Evaluation, U.S. Department of Education, by Pelavin Associates, Inc., Washington, D.C., p. 70.

4. Ibid., p. 5.

5. Ibid., pp. 6–13; Rita Kirshstein et al., "Years Two and Three of the Chelsea-BU Partnership: A Story of Survival," Pelavin Associates, Inc., Washington, D.C., 1994.

6. Glenn Jacobs, "History, Crisis, and Social Panic: Minority Resistance to Privatization of an Urban School System," *Urban Review* 25, no. 3 (September 1993): 175–98.

7. Cited in ibid., p. 184.

8. Pelavin, Siegel, and Kirshstein, "Implementation of the Chelsea School Project," p. 8.

9. Ibid., pp. vii, 74.

10. "Urban School Reform: Persistence Starts to Pay Off," report, A Different September Foundation, Chelsea, Mass., Fall 1994.

11. Kirshstein et al., "Years Two and Three of the Chelsea-BU Partnership," p. 7.

12. The Massachusetts Proposition 2 1/2 legislation caps local tax assessment on real estate and personal property at 2.5 percent per year, but localities can override the legislation for a given year.

13. "Urban School Reform," p. 16.

14. Kirshstein et al., "Years Two and Three of the Chelsea-BU Partnership," p. 31.

15. Ibid., p. 61.

16. "Urban School Reform." The report also cited a 50 percent increase in the number of students pursuing postsecondary education.

17. Kirshstein et al., "Years Two and Three of the Chelsea-BU Partnership," pp. 22–23.

18. Ibid., p. 14.

19. Ibid., p. 87.

20. A. Bilik, "Privatization: Selling America to the Lowest Bidder," *Labor Research Review* 9 (Spring 1990): 6–7; cited in Jacobs, "History, Crisis, and Social Panic," p. 178.

21. Pelavin, Siegel, and Kirshstein, "Implementation of the Chelsea School Project," p. 10.

22. Kirshstein et al., "Years Two and Three of the Chelsea-BU Partnership," p. 13.

23. "Urban School Reform," p. 2.

24. K. R. Lampke, "Mayor Sees End of Urban Schools," *Milwaukee Sentinel*, p. 1.

25. Thomas Hetland, "The Milwaukee Choice Program," in Simon Hakim, Paul Seidenstat, and Gary W. Bowman, eds., *Privatizing Education and Educational Choice: Concepts, Plans and Experiences* (Westport, Conn.: Praeger, 1994), pp. 183–89.

26. This section is based on John F. Witte et al., "Fourth-Year Report: Milwaukee Parental Choice Program," Department of Political Science and the Robert La Follette Institute of Public Affairs, University of Wisconsin-Madison, December 1994.

27. Cheryl Gamble, "2 schools in Milwaukee Choice Program Close," *Education Week*, February 21, 1996, p. 3.

28. Ibid., p. 3.

29. For examples of alternative interpretations, see Daniel McGroarty, "School Choice Slandered," *Public Interest*, Fall 1994, pp. 94–111; and Paul E. Peterson, "A Critique of the Witte Evaluation of the Milwaukee's School Choice Program," Center for American Political Studies, Harvard University, February 1995. A more recent reanalysis is by Jay P. Greene, Paul E. Peterson, and Jiangto Du, "The Effectiveness of School Choice in Milwaukee: A Secondary Analysis of Data from the Program's Evaluation," University of Houston and Harvard University. This paper, presented at the Meetings of the American Political Science Association, San Francisco, Cal., August 30, 1996, has been criticized for its methadology and been the subject of some controversy.

30. See the achievement results in Witte et al., "Fourth-Year Report," pp. 13–19.

31. Ibid., p. v.

32. Ibid.

33. Ibid, p. 18.

34. Ibid.

35. Ibid., p. 19.

36. John F. Witte, "Who Benefits from the Milwaukee Choice Program?" in Bruce Fuller et al., eds., *Who Chooses? Who Loses? Culture, Institutions, and the Unequal Effects of School Choice* (New York: Teachers College Press, 1996), p. 133.

37. Ibid., p. 1.

38. U.S. Department of Commerce, Bureau of the Census, *Public Education Finances: 1990–91*, Series GF/91-10 (Washington, D.C.: U.S. Government Printing Office, 1993), pp. 78–79.

39. Witte et al., "Fourth-Year Report," Appendix B, p. 14.

40. Ibid., Appendix B, p. 19.

41. Gamble, "2 Schools in Milwaukee Choice Program Close."

42. Witte et al., "Fourth-Year Report," p. 20.

43. Witte et al., "Fourth-Year Report," p. 5.

44. Ibid., Table 4.

45. Ibid., p. 8.

46. Ibid., p. 26.

47. Ibid., p. 10.

48. Ibid., Appendix C, p. 21.

49. Ibid., p. 29.

50. Ibid., Appendix C, p. 21.

51. Ibid., p. iii.

52. William H. Miller, "Teaching Johnny, Corporate Style," *Industry Week*, May 7, 1990, p. 39.

53. Corporate/Community Schools of America, "Progress Report, 1988–89," ERIC Document 311 #104, Chicago, June 1989.

54. Carol Bentley, "America's First Corporate School: Model for Educational Reform?" paper presented at the annual meeting of the Mid-Western Educational Research Association, Chicago, October 17–20, 1990, ERIC Document 333 #536.

55. Ibid.

56. Steve Weiner, "We Decided to Show How Things Can Work," pp. 180–88.

57. Ibid., p. 188.

58. Ibid., p. 184.

59. Bentley, "America's First Corporate School."

60. A. David, "Public-Private Partnerships: The Private Sector and Innovation in Education, *Policy Insight*, no. 142 (1992).

61. Bentley, "America's First Corporate School," p. 8.

62. Telephone interviews by Carol Ascher with Raelinne Toperoff and Coleen Maia, former teachers at the Chicago Corporate Community School, April 15, 1996.

63. Anne Hallett, personal communication with the authors, December 21, 1994.

64. Kathy Evans and Ted Carroll, "Why We Did It: Two Hartford Board Members Explain the Decision to Go Private," *American School Board Journal*, March 1995, p. 44.

65. "Hartford School Board Scales Back Privatization Plan," *School Board News*, June 27, 1995, p. 5.

66. George Judson, "Private Business, Public Schools: Why Hartford Experiment Failed," *New York Times*, March 11, 1996, pp. A1, B5; this section relies heavily on Judson's in-depth article, which does an excellent job of telling the whole story of EAI in Hartford; all facts not otherwise footnoted are from Judson's piece.

67. Rick Green, "EAI Wins Vote to Run Hartford Schools," *Hartford Courant*, July 23, 1994, pp. A1, A5.

68. Peter Schmidt, "Hartford Asks E.A.I. to Help Run Its District," *Education Week*, August 3, 1994, pp. 1, 19.

69. Peter Schmidt, "Hartford Hires E.A.I. to Run Entire District," *Education Week*, October 12, 1994, pp. 1, 14.

70. News release, "Hartford Public Schools and the *Alliance for Schools that Work* Form Groundbreaking Public-Private Partnership," Education Alternatives, Inc., Minneapolis, October 3, 1994.

71. George Judson, "Hartford Schools Enter New World," *New York Times*, March 9, 1995, p. B6.

72. Evans and Carroll, "Why We Did It," p. 44.

73. Green, "EAI Wins Vote to Run Hartford Schools."

74. Rick Green, "100 Days Later, Plenty of Praise for EAI," *Hartford Courant*, March 7, 1995, pp. B1, B2.

75. Judson, "Hartford Schools Enter New World."

76. Judson, "Private Business, Public Schools."

77. Ibid.

78. Peter Schmidt, "Attacks Mount against E.A.I.'s Hartford Plans," *Education Week*, May 24, 1995, pp. 1, 10, 11.

79. Ibid., p. 10.

80. Ibid., p. 11.

81. Ibid., p. 10.

82. See Kirk Johnson, "Hartford to Slow Company Role in Schools," *New York Times*, June 21, 1995, p. B5. See also "Hartford School Board Scales Back Privatization Plan."

83. "Hartford School Board Scales Back Privatization Plan."

84 Johnson, "Hartford to Slow Company Role in Schools"; also see "Hartford School Board Scales Back Privatization Plan."

85 Mark Walsh, "Hartford Ousts EAI in Dispute over Finances," *Education Week*, January 31, 1996, pp. 1, 9.

86. Cheryl Gamble, "Hartford Officials Agree to Pay EAI $3 Million," *Education Week*, January 10, 1996, p. 7.

87. Ibid.

88. Ibid.

89. Walsh, "Hartford Ousts EAI in Dispute over Finances," p. 9.

90. Ibid., pp. 1, 9.

91. Mark Walsh, "Hartford City Officials Float Plan to Keep EAI on in Financial Role," *Education Week*, February 14, 1996, p. 6.

92. "Hartford Agrees to Pay E.A.I. for Computers, Equipment," *Education Week*, June 5, 1996, p. 4.

93. Ann Bradley, "Hartford Council Seeks State Help in Running Schools," *Education Week*, May 22, 1996, p. 3.

94. John Larrabee, "The Business of School Reform," *USA Today*, June 7, 1995, p. 1.

6.

1. Benjamin R. Barber, "Workshops of Our Democracy," *Education Week*, April 19, 1995, p. 34.

2. Arthur E. Wise, *Legislated Learning: The Bureaucratization of the American Classroom* (Berkeley, Calif.: University of California Press, 1979).

3. Susan McAllister Swap, "Can Parent Involvement Lead to Increased Student Achievement in Urban Schools?" ERIC Document ED 333 #079, 1991.

4. Jonathan Kozol, *Savage Inequalities: Children in America's Schools* (New York: Crown Publishers, 1991).

5. Michelle Fine, *Framing Dropouts: Notes on the Politics of an Urban Public High School* (Albany: State University of New York, 1991).

6. Ibid.

7. Gerald Bracey, "The Third Bracey Report," *Phi Delta Kappan*, October 1993, pp. 105–16.

8. Larry E. Suter, ed., *Indicators of Science and Mathematics Education, 1995* (Arlington, Va.: National Science Foundation, 1996).

9. David Grissmer et al., *Student Achievement and the Changing Family* (Santa Monica, Calif.: RAND Corporation, 1995).

10. Bracey, "The Third Bracey Report."

11. David C. Berliner and Bruce J. Biddle, *The Manufactured Crisis: Myths, Fraud and the Attack on America's Public Schools* (Reading, Mass.: Addison-Wesley, 1995).

12. Ibid.

13. Bracey, "The Third Bracey Report."

14. Ibid.

15. W. T. Grant Commission on Work, Family, and Citizenship, *The Forgotten Half: Pathways to Success for America's Youth* (Washington, D.C.: W. T. Grant Foundation, 1988).

16. See, for example, Chester E. Finn, Jr., "The High School Dropout Puzzle," *Public Interest*, Spring 1987, pp. 3–22.

17. Anne Wheelock, *Crossing the Tracks: How "Untracking" Can Save America's Schools* (New York: New Press, 1992); Jeannie Oakes, *Keeping Track: How Schools Structure Inequality* (New Haven: Yale University Press, 1985).

18. Diane Ravitch, *National Standards in American Education: A Citizen's Guide* (Washington, D.C.: Brookings Institution, 1995).

19. See Ted Sizer, *Horace's Compromises: The Dilemma of the American High School* (Boston: Houghton Mifflin, 1992); Ted Sizer, *Horace's School: Redesigning the American High School* (Boston, Houghton Mifflin, 1992); and Deborah Meier, *The Power of Their Ideas* (Boston: Beacon Press, 1995).

20. Peter Applebome, "Education Summit Calls for Tough Standards to Be Set by States and Local School Districts," *New York Times*, March 27, 1996, p. B9; see also American Federation of Teachers, "Making Standards Matter," in *Do We Still Need Public Schools?* (Washington, D.C.: *Phi Delta Kappan* and Center on National Education Policy, 1996).

21. Futures Committee, Coalition of Essential Schools, *Looking to the Future: From Conversation to Demonstration* (Providence: Coalition of Essential Schools, November 1995).

22. Sue Lehmann and Evan Spring, "High Academic Standards and School Reform: Education Leaders Speak Out," in *1996 National Education Summit*, Governors' and Business Leaders' National Education Goals Panel, New York, November 1995.

23. John E. Chubb and Terry M. Moe, *Politics, Markets and America's Schools* (Washington, D.C.: Brookings Institution, 1990), p. 217.

24. Harold L. Hodgkinson, *A Demographic Look at Tomorrow* (Washington, D.C.: Center for Demographic Policy, Institute for Educational Leadership, 1992).

25. Joy G. Dryfoos, *Full Service Schools: A Revolution in Health and Social Services for Children, Youth and Families* (San Francisco: Jossey-Bass, 1994).

26. David Seeley et al., "Restructuring Schools [and] School Leadership: Improving Inner City Elementary Schools, Report on Interviews with 25 New York City Principals," report no. 1, City University of New York Research Foundation, 1990.

27. Harold L. Hodgkinson, *Bringing Tomorrow into Focus* (Washington, D.C.: Center for Demographic Policy, Institute for Educational Leadership, 1996).

28. *The Unfinished Journey: Restructuring Schools in a Diverse Society*, California Tomorrow, San Francisco, 1994; see also "Drawing Strength from Diversity: Effective Services for Children, Youth and Families," report, California Tomorrow, San Francisco, 1996.

29. National School Boards Association, *Private Options for Public Schools: Ways Public Schools Are Exploring Privatization* (Reston, Va.: National School Boards Association, 1995).

30. Ibid.

31. David Tyack and Larry Cuban, *Tinkering toward Utopia: A Century of Public School Reform* (Cambridge, Mass.: Harvard University Press, 1995).

32. Kristen J. Amundson, "Restructuring, Reform and Reality: What School Districts Are Really Doing," NSBA Best Practices Series, National School Boards Association, Alexandria, Va., 1993.

33. "Reform Data Book," *Catalyst: Voices of Chicago School Reform*, Fifth Anniversary Issue 6, no. 5 (February 1995): 27–38.

34. Fred Hess, "School Restructuring, Chicago Style: A Midway Report," Chicago Panel on Public School Policy and Finance, Chicago, February 1992; "Reform Data Book."

35. "School-Based Budget Training Project," Cross City Campaign for Urban School Reform, Chicago, May 1996.

36. Mitchell Korn, *Institutionalizing Arts Education for NYC Public Schools: Educational Improvement and Reform through the Arts* (New York: Arts Vision, 1995).

37. *Tomorrow's Teacher: A Report of the Holmes Group* (East Lansing, Mich.: Holmes Group, 1986); and James Banks, Linda Darling-Hammond, and Maxine Greene, *Building Learner-Centered Schools: Three Perspectives* (New York: National Center for Restructuring Education, Schools, and Teaching, Columbia University Teachers' College, 1992).

38. Norm Fruchter and Michele Cahill, *School Reform through Collaboration: Contract for America's Youth* (Washington, D.C.: Academy for Educational Development, 1994).

39. J. Lawrence Aber, "Evaluation of the Resolving Conflict Creatively Program: An Overview," special supplement, *American Journal of Preventive Medicine*, Fall 1996.

40. "Budget Operations and Review Memorandum no. 1: FY 94–95," New York City Board of Education, July 1994.

41. Norm Fruchter et al., "Focus on Learning: A Report on Reorganizing General and Special Education in New York City," Institute for Education and Social Policy, New York University, 1995.

42. Thomas B. Parrish and Deborah A. Verstegen, "Fiscal Provisions of the Individuals with Disabilities Education Act: Policy Issues and Alternatives," policy paper no. 3, Center for Special Education Finance, American Institute for Research, Palo Alto, Calif., 1994.

43. Jennifer Hochschild, *Facing Up to the American Dream: Race, Class and the Soul of the Nation* (Princeton, N.J.: Princeton University Press, 1995).

44. Ibid.; see also Gary Orfield and Susan E. Eaton, *Dismantling Desegregation: The Quiet Reversal of Brown vs. Board of Education* (New York: New Press, 1996).

45. Louann A. Bierlein, *Charter Schools: Initial Findings* (Denver: Education Commission of the States, 1996).

46. *School Choice: A Special Report* (Ewing, N.J.: Carnegie Foundation on Teaching, 1992).

47. Ann Henderson, *Beyond the Bake Sale* (Washington, D.C.: National Committee for Citizens in Education, 1986).

48. "Reform Data Book."

49. Norm Fruchter, Anne Galletta, and J. L. White, *New Directions in Parent Involvement* (Washington, D.C.: Academy for Educational Development, 1992).

50. Ibid.

51. David Tyack, *The One Best System* (Cambridge, Mass.: Harvard University Press, 1974).

52. Robert Berne and Lawrence O. Picus, *Outcome Equity in Education* (Thousand Oaks, Calif.: Corwin Press, 1994).

53. Jessica Siegel, "After the Fall," *Teacher Magazine*, March 1994.

54. "Implementing Performance Assessments: A Guide to Classroom, School and System Reform," FairTest/The National Center for Fair and Open Testing, Cambridge, Mass., 1995.

55. Chubb and Moe, *Politics, Markets and America's Schools.*

56. Norm Fruchter and Robert Berne, "A Modest Proposal for Improving New York State's Educational Outcomes, in Effective Government Now for the New Century: The Final Report of the Temporary State Commission on Constitutional Revision," mimeograph (New York: Institute for Education and Social Policy, 1995).

57. James S. Coleman, Thomas Hoffer, and Sally Kilgore, *High School Achievement: Public, Catholic, and Private Schools Compared* (New York: Basic Books, 1982); Anthony S. Bryk, Valerie E. Lee, and Peter Holland, *Catholic Schools and the Common Good* (Cambridge, Mass.: Harvard University Press, 1993).

58. "Rethinking Central Office," Cross City Campaign for Urban School Reform, Chicago, 1994.

59. "Reform Data Book."

60. "New York City School Governance," report prepared by the Fund for New York City Public Education, New York, February 1996.

61. Joseph B. Shedd and S. B. Bachrach, *Tangled Hierarchies: Teachers as Professionals and the Management of Schools* (San Francisco: Jossey-Bass, 1991).

62. Berne and Picus, *Outcome Equity in Education.*

63. Hochschild, *Facing Up to the American Dream.*

64. Gary Orfield and Susan E. Eaton, *Dismantling Desegregation: The Quiet Reversal of Brown vs. Board of Education* (New York: New Press, 1996).

65. Ibid.

66. Derrick Bell, *And We Are Not Saved: The Elusive Quest for Racial Justice* (New York: Basic Books, 1987); William J. Wilson, *The Ghetto Underclass* (Newbury Park, Calif.: Sage Publications, 1993).

67. See, for example, Carol Ascher, "Efficiency, Equity, and Local Control—School Finance in Texas," *ERIC Clearinghouse on Urban Education DIGEST* (New York), no. 88 (April 1993); Carol Ascher, "Urban School Finance: The Quest for Equal Educational Opportunity," *ERIC Clearinghouse on Urban Education DIGEST* (New York), no. 55 (1989).

68. Michael A. Rebell, "Fiscal Equity in Education: Deconstructing the Reigning Myths and Facing Reality," *New York University Review of Law and Social Change* 21, no. 4 (1994–95): 691–723.

69. Marilyn Gittell and Kirk Vandersall, "Regimes and Reform: State Politics and Urban School Reform," preliminary report, Howard Samuels Center, City University of New York Graduate School, June 1996.

70. While this point of view has been expressed by a range of politicians, including former President George Bush, the study most often cited in behalf of the "money doesn't matter" argument is E. A. Hanushek, "The Impact of Differential Expenditures on School Performance," *Educational Researcher*, May 1989, pp. 47–51.

71. Meier, *Power of Their Ideas*, p. 7.

72. Ibid., p. 7.

73. Hodgkinson, *Demographic Look at Tomorrow.*

74. This quote is used in "Teaching Democracy: Defining the Role of Public Education in a Civil Society," *Education Week*, April 19, 1995, p. 33.

75. Bill Bigelow, in *Rethinking Columbus: Special Issue*, Rethinking Schools, Milwaukee, 1992.

76. Todd Gitlin, *The Twilight of Common Dreams: Why America Is Wracked by Culture Wars* (New York: Metropolitan Books, 1995).

7.

1. Don Cameron, "Preserving the American Dream: Toward a Recommitment to Public Education in America," *Educational Horizons* 71, no. 1 (Fall 1992): 32.

2. William K. Cummings and Abbey Riddell, "Alternative Policies for the Finance, Control and Delivery of Basic Education," *International Journal of Educational Research* 21, no. 8 (1994): 751–828.

3. John Silber, president of Boston University, quoted in Rita Kirshstein et al., "Years Two and Three of the Chelsea-BU Partnership: A Story of Survival," Pelavin Associates, Inc., Washington, D.C., 1994, p. 1.

4. Bruce Fuller et al., eds., *Who Chooses? Who Loses? Culture, Institutions, and the Unequal Effects of School Choice* (New York: Teachers College Press, 1996).

5. Louann Bierlein, at a Panel Discussion on Charter Schools sponsored by the Center for Educational Innovation, New York Democratic Leadership Council Working Group on School Organization and Educational Quality, Harvard Club, New York, February 2, 1996.

6. *Congressional Quarterly Researcher*, March 25, 1994, quoted in *The Private Management of Public Schools: An Analysis of the EAI Experience in Baltimore*, report, American Federation of Teachers, Washington, D.C., May 1994.

7. Fuller, *Who Chooses? Who Loses?*

8. Lois C. Williams and Lawrence E. Leak, *The UMBC Evaluation of the Tesseract Program in Baltimore City*, report, Center for Educational Research, University of Maryland, Baltimore County, September 1, 1995.

9. James T. Bennett and Manuel H. Johnson, *Better Government at Half the Price: Private Production of Public Services* (Aurora, Ill.: Caroline House Publishers, 1981).

10. Robert Berne, "The Effects of Size on School Costs in New York City High Schools: Conceptual Issues," draft, Institute for Education and Social Policy, New York University, January 1996.

11. Mary B. W. Tabor, "Investors Look to Education as Possibility for High Flier," *New York Times*, May 29, 1996, p. B9.

12. Henry M. Levin, "The Economics of Choice," *Economics of Education Review* 10, no. 2 (1991): 137–58.

Index

Abell Foundation, 44, 121n. 8
Accelerated Schools, 87, 92
Accountability, 11, 16–17; and
BCPS, 54–55, 109; bureaucratic,
94–95; and charter schools, 22; and
Chelsea-BU Partnership, 68–69; fis-
cal, 93–94; and for-profit corpora-
tions, 8; and Milwaukee Choice
Program, 73–74; and performance
contracting, 24; and privatization,
109–10; and public authority, 6;
and public education, 93–95
Adult Basic Education Program
(Chelsea), 67
Africa, 101
AFT. *See* American Federation of
Teachers
Alabama, 96
Alliance for Schools that Work, 77
Alum Rock experiment, 39–41,
101–3; and equity, 110–11
American Association of Educators in
Private Practice, 21
American College Testing (ACT), 84
*American Education: The Dynamics of
Choice* (Reinhard and Lee), 18
American Federation of Teachers
(AFT), 87; and EAI schools, 45,
47–48, 77
Amprey, Walter G., 44, 45, 48
Arizona: and school choice, 15

Baltimore, 6, 96; and EAI, 106, 108,
111
Baltimore City Public Schools
(BCPS) system, 43–44, 95, 101,
108; and accountability, 54–55,
109; and cost, 52–53; Department
of Research and Evaluation, 46–47;
and EAI, 7–8, 44–59, 81, 105; and
educational outcomes, 50–52, 104;
and equity, 55; and parental voice,
53–54; and Tesseract Program, 17,
45–59, 106; and University of
Maryland evaluation report, 49–57
Baltimore Teachers Union (BTU),
46, 47, 48, 50, 58
Bannecker Elementary School experi-
ment: and performance contracting,
30–34; and staffing, 35
Barber, Benjamin, R., 83
Barclay-Calvert Program, 121n. 8
Batelle Laboratories, 29
BCPS. *See* Baltimore City Public
Schools (BCPS) system
Beales, Janet, 15, 21–22
Behavioral Research Laboratories
(BRL), 31–34
Bennett, David, 17
Bennett, William, 5
BERRI, 44
*Better Government at Half the Price!
Private Production of Public Services*, 21

Beyond Public Education (Lieberman), 16

Boston University, 6, 65, 82, 103, 106, 109. *See also* Chelsea-Boston University Partnership

Bowman, Gary, 22

"Break-the-mold" classrooms, 8

BRL (Behavioral Research Laboratories), 31–34

Bronx High School of Science, 91

Brookings Institution study, 30

Brooklyn, 31

Brown v. Board of Education, 2, 83, 95, 112

BTU. *See* Baltimore Teachers Union

Bush, George, 132n. 70; and school prayer, 5

Business: and school efficiency, 21

Busing, 2, 18

California: and performance contracting, 27, 28

Calvert School, 121n. 8

Cambridge, Massachusetts, 92

Cameron, Don, 99

Caribbean, 97

Carnegie Foundation, 15

Carroll, Ted, 77

Catholic groups: and vouchers, 5

Catholic schools, 94; costs, 10; and diversity, 20

CCSA (Corporate Community Schools of America), 74–76

Central America, 97

Central Europe, 100

Central High School (Philadelphia), 91

Challenge Schools program, 44

Charter school movement, 6, 22

Charter schools, 7, 92

Chelsea, 6, 81, 82, 96, 103

Chelsea-Boston University Partnership, 62–66, 88, 109; and accountability, 68–69; and cost, 66–67, 106; and educational

outcomes, 66, 105; and equity, 69; and parental voice, 67, 108

Chelsea Executive Advisory Committee (CEAC), 67

Cherry Creek, Colorado: and performance contracting, 28

Chicago, 89–90, 92, 95; and performance contracting, 28

Chicago Board of Education, 76

Chicago Corporate Community School, 74–76, 81, 88, 103, 111; and accountability, 109; and cost, 106

Chicago public schools, 75–76, 103; and cost, 106

China, 97

Choice. *See* School choice

Choice in Schooling: A Case for Tuition Vouchers (Kirkpatrick), 20

Christian fundamentalists, 20

Christian values, 4–5

Chubb, John, 16–17, 88; and diversity, 20

Churchill, Winston, 98

Cincinnati, 95

City governments: privatized functions of, 6

Civic consciousness, 4

Clarke, Mary Pat, 123n. 46

Coalition of Essential Schools, 87

Cohen, David K., 40

Colorado Department of Education, 27

Common culture, 20

Comprehensive Test of Basic Skills (CTBS), 51

Computer Curriculum Company (CCC), 45, 47, 77

Congress, 30, 87

Conservative groups, 4–5; and accountability, 6

Contracting out: and public education, 89–90

Contract schools: and equity, 19

Control Data Corporation, 44

Corporate Community Schools of America (CCSA), 74–76
Cost, 4, 10–11, 21–22; and BCPS, 52–53; and Chelsea-BU Partnership, 66–67, 106; and EAI, 46–47, 58–59, 123n. 61, 123n. 62; and Milwaukee Choice Program, 71–72; and performance contracting, 36–37; and privatization, 106–8; and public education, 88–91. *See also* Financing
Cross-district choice programs, 92

Dade County (Florida), 6, 31, 44
Dallas: and performance contracting, 28
Davis, Eddie L., 77, 79, 81
Department of Defense, 24
Department of Health, Education and Welfare, 28, 30
Department of Research and Evaluation (Baltimore), 46–47, 49
Desegregation, 2, 17–18; and public education, 95–96
Different September Foundation, A, 63, 64, 66, 69
Diversity, 20–21
Dorsett Educational Systems, Inc., 25–26, 36
Dorsett Rapid Learning Centers, 25–26
Doyle, Denis, 13, 16
Dunbar Project, 121n. 8

Eagan, Minnesota, 44
EAI, 7–8, 13, 37, 101, 109; and AFT, 47–48, 77; and Baltimore, 44–59, 105, 106, 108; and cost, 46–47, 58–59, 123n. 61, 123n. 62; and educational outcomes, 58; and equity, 111; and Hartford, 76–81, 82, 103, 106; and parental voice, 124n. 67; and Tesseract Program, 105
Early Learning Center (Chelsea), 63, 65

Eastern Europe, 97, 100
Edison Project, The, 20
Educational Alliance, 45
Educational Development Laboratories, Inc. (EDL), 26–27
Educational for All Handicapped Act, 74
Educational outcomes, 10; and BCPS, 50–52, 104; and Chelsea-BU Partnership, 66, 105; and EAI, 58; and Milwaukee Choice Program, 70–71; and privatization, 104–6; and public education, 84–88
Educational productivity, 8
Education Alternatives, Inc. *See* EAI
Educational Testing Service, 26
Education industry stock index, 13
Education Investor, The, 13, 19
Efficiency, school, 21–22
Elementary and Secondary Education Act (ESEA), 24, 25, 26
Embry, Robert C., Jr., 121n. 8
Emergency School Aid Act (ESAA), 18
Equality, 17–21
Equity, 2, 3, 11–12; and BCPS, 55; and Chelsea-BU Partnership, 69; and for-profit corporations, 8; and Milwaukee Choice Program, 74; and privatization, 110–11; and public education, 95–97
ESAA (Emergency School Aid Act), 18
ESEA (Elementary and Secondary Education Act), 24, 25, 26
Europe, 100
Evans, Kathy, 77

Family-School Partnership, 44
Farrar, Eleanor, 40
Financial Oversight Committee (EAI), 49
Financing, 3, 10; and equity, 19, 96–97. *See also* Cost
Finn, Chester, 14, 17

Flag, honoring the, 5
Flint, Michigan: and performance contracting, 27
Follow Through, 28
For-profit corporations, 7–8
For-profit organizations, 22
For-profit schools, 20
"Fourth-Year Report" (Milwaukee), 70, 74
Franzi, Gary, 79
Free schools, 2
Friedman, Milton, 5; and vouchers, 38
Fund for Educational Excellence, 44

GAO (General Accounting Office), 30, 43, 109; and EAI accountability, 55; and EAI costs, 53
Gary, Indiana, 102; and performance contracting, 27, 28, 31–34
Gawrys, John, 64
Gilroy, California: and performance contracting, 28
Goins, William, 79
Golle, John, 43, 57, 79, 80, 104
Governance: and performance contracting, 35–36
Government: privatized functions of, 6; and school efficiency, 21; sentiment against, 4
Grand Rapids: and performance contracting, 28
Great Britain, 100
Greer, Peter, 63, 64

Hakim, Simon, 22
Hartford, 6, 101; and accountability, 109; and EAI, 76–81, 82, 103, 106, 111
Hartford Courant, 78
Harvard University, 71
Head Start, 24, 28
Health Care, Counseling and Coordination Center (Chelsea), 64, 65
Henig, Jeffrey, 9
High Technology Home Daycare Project, 66

Hill, Paul, 16, 17; and contract schools, 19
HIPPY (Home Instruction Program for Preschool Youth), 66, 67
Home Instruction Program for Preschool Youth (HIPPY), 66, 67

Illinois, 95
Immigration: and public education, 9
Indiana General Education Commission, 32
Indian subcontinent, 97
Instructional methods: and performance contracting, 34–35, 37–38
Intergenerational Literacy Project (Chelsea), 67
International Association for the Evaluation of Educational Achievement, 86
Iowa: and school choice, 15

Jacksonville: and performance contracting, 28
Jacobs, Glenn, 63
Jencks, Christopher, 23; and vouchers, 38–39
Johnson, Lyndon, 23, 28
Johnson Controls, 45, 77

Kellerman, Joseph, 61, 74, 75
Kentucky, 90, 95, 96
Kirkpatrick, David, 20
KPMG Peat Marwick, 45, 77

Lam, Diana, 63, 64
Latin America, 101
Learning Foundations, 30
Lee, Jackson F., 18
Lehman Brothers, 82
Lessinger, Leon, 24
Lieberman, Myron, 16, 19, 30; and diversity, 20

Magnet schools: and equity, 18
Manhattan's District 4, 91–92

Market mechanisms, 8, 17
Maryland Education Department, 48
Maryland School Performance
    Assessment Program, 51, 57
Maryland State Board of Education,
    121n. 8
Massachusetts: Proposition 2 1/2, 64,
    125n.12
Massachusetts General
    Hospital/Chelsea Memorial Health
    Center, 65
McLaughlin, John, 13, 19
Meier, Deborah, 97
Miami-Dade County public school
    district, 44
Michigan: and performance contract-
    ing, 27
Milliken decision, 91
Milwaukee, 6, 96, 102, 103, 108; and
    cost, 106
Milwaukee Choice Program, 69–74, 81;
    and accountability, 73–74, 110; and
    cost, 71–72; and educational out-
    comes, 70–71, 104; and equity, 74,
    110, 111; and parental voice, 72–73
Milwaukee Public Schools, 69–74
Minneapolis, 6, 89, 106
Model Cities, 25
Moe, Michael, 82, 88
Moe, Terry, 16–17; and diversity, 20
Monroe, Michigan: and performance
    contracting, 32
Montclair, New Jersey, 92

National Assessment of Educational
    Progress (NAEP), 84–85
National Science Foundation report,
    85
Nation at Risk, A, 2, 86
New Jersey, 93
New York, 93, 96
New York City, 89, 91–92, 95
New York Times, 77
Nixon, Richard, 23–24, 28
Noguera, Pedro A., 1

Nonprofit institutions, 8
Norquist, John O., 69

OEO (Office of Educational
    Opportunity), 23, 34; and cost, 37;
    and instructional methods, 35; and
    performance contracting, 26, 27,
    28–30; and staffing, 35; and vouch-
    er experiment, 39–40
Office of Education, 23, 24; and per-
    formance contracting, 25
Office of Educational Opportunity.
    See OEO
O'Leary, John, 15
Outcomes. *See* Educational outcomes

Paradise Valley, Arizona, 44
Parental voice, 11, 16–17; and BCPS,
    53–54; and Chelsea-BU
    Partnership, 67, 108; and EAI,
    124n. 67; and Milwaukee Choice
    Program, 72–73; and performance
    contracting, 36; and privatization,
    108; and public education, 91–93
Parent Information Center (Chelsea),
    63–64, 67
Pelavin Associates, 64, 65, 68
Performance contracting, 17, 23–24,
    41–42; and Bannecker Elementary
    School, 30–34; and cost, 36–37;
    and governance, 35–36; and in-
    structional methods, 34–35, 37–38;
    and OEO, 26, 27, 28–30; and
    parental voice, 36; spread of, 27–28;
    and staffing, 35; and testing, 36;
    and Texarkana, Arkansas, 24–27
Peters, Michael, 80, 81
Phi Delta Kappan/Gallup education
    poll, 2, 3
Philadelphia, 91; and performance
    contracting, 27, 32
Philippines, 97
Politics, Markets, and America's Schools
    (Moe and Chubb), 16–17
Porter, Judson, 45

Portland, Oregon: and performance
    contracting, 27
Prayer, school, 5
"Private Management of Public
    Schools: An Analysis of the EAI
    Experience in Baltimore," 47
Privatization: and accountability,
    109–10; and cost, 106–8; definition
    of, 6–7; and educational outcomes,
    104–6; and equity, 110–11; experi-
    ment results, 101–4; and parental
    voice, 108; problems with, 111–13;
    vs. public education, 99–101
Privatization and Educational Choice
    (Lieberman), 19
Proposition 2 1/2, 64, 125n.12
Public Agenda, 2
Public authority, 6
Public education, 83–84, 97–98; and
    accountability, 93–95; and contract-
    ing out ancillary systems, 89–90; and
    cost, 88–91; and desegregation,
    95–96; and educational outcomes,
    84–88; and equalization in funding,
    96–97; and equity, 95–97; and
    instructional costs, 90–91; and
    parental voice, 91–93; and school
    choice, 91–93; vs. privatization,
    99–101
Public engagement, 4
Public schools: privatized functions
    of, 6
Public Strategies, Inc., 6, 106

Quality Education Development
    Corporation, 30
Race, 17
Rader, Don, 26
RAND Corporation, 30
RAND evaluation, 32
RAND study, 85
Reagan, Ronald: and school prayer, 5
Reason Foundation, 15, 21
Reinhard, James, 18

Religious groups, 4–5; and diversity,
    20; and vouchers, 5
Religious schools, 10, 94; and diversi-
    ty, 20
Robinson v. Cahill, 95
Rochester, 95
Roosevelt (Long Island) school dis-
    trict, 93

Salaries, teacher, 22
Schmoke, Kurt, 2, 43–44, 48–49, 57,
    120n. 5, 123n. 46
Scholastic Aptitude Test (SAT), 84–85
School choice, 7, 11; and Carnegie
    Foundation, 15; and Chubb and
    Moe, 16–17; and public education,
    91–93
School Choice reports (Carnegie
    Foundation), 15
School Development Program, 87, 92
School efficiency, 21–22
School prayer, 5
Seattle, 95
Seidenstat, Paul, 22
Sequoia Institute, 40
Serano v. Priest, 95
Shanker, Albert, 62
Shareholders, 10–11
Silber, John, 62, 63
Singer/Graflex, 30
Slavin, Robert, 44
Social class, 18–19
South America, 97
Southeast Asia, 97
South Pointe Elementary School
    (Miami-Dade County), 44
Soviet Union, former, 97, 100
St. Louis: and school choice, 15
Staffing: and performance contract-
    ing, 35
Standards, 2
Student achievement, 14–16
Stuyvesant High School (New York),
    91

Success for All, 44, 92, 121n. 8
SuccessMaker instructional technology, 45, 46, 47, 78
Sullivan, William, 31–32, 33

Tax credits, 6–7
Tax revenues, 3
Teacher certification, 22
Teachers Involve Parents in Schoolwork (TIPS), 44
Teachers' unions, 22
Television, 20
Tesseract Program, 105, 108, 124n. 67; and Baltimore, 17, 45–59, 106; and Hartford, 78; and Miami-Dade County public school district, 44
Testing: and performance contracting, 36
Test scores: and BCPS, 50–51; and public education, 84–85
Texarkana, Arkansas, 34; and performance contracting, 24–27, 28; and testing, 36
TIPS (Teachers Involve Parents in Schoolwork), 44
Toledo, 95
Traditional values, 4–5
Transportation: and vouchers, 18

UMBC (University of Maryland-Baltimore County) evaluation, 49–57
Unions: and EAI, 59; sentiment against, 4
Unions, teachers', 22

University of Houston, 71
University of Maryland, 48, 105; and Baltimore County evaluation report, 49–57
"Urban School Reform," 64
Urban schools, 3, 4; privatization efforts in, 8
U.S. Department of Education: and EAI schools, 48

Vietnam War, 24
Virginia: and free schools, 2; and performance contracting, 27
Vouchers, 5, 6, 7, 23–24, 38–39, 42; and Alum Rock experiment, 39–41; and Chubb and Moe, 17; and equity, 18, 19

Walsh, Norman J., 45
Westinghouse Learning Corporation, 30
White Plains, New York, 92
Whittle, Chris, 14, 20, 21
Wichita: and performance contracting, 28
Wisconsin Department of Public Instruction, 74
Witte, John, 70, 71, 73

"Years Two and Three of the Chelsea-BU Partnership," 64, 66, 68, 125n. 16
Yelich, Chris, 21

ABOUT THE AUTHORS

Carol Ascher is senior research associate at New York University's Institute for Education and Social Policy, an interdisciplinary policy institute committed to improving urban schools. Between 1979 and 1994, she was senior research associate at the ERIC Clearinghouse on Urban Education and Institute for Urban and Minority Education at Columbia Teachers College. She has written numerous monographs and articles on urban education. Most recently, her review of issues relating to school choice and to the 1970s experiment in performance contracting appeared in *The Harvard Education Review* and *Phi Delta Kappan*, respectively. She is also a well-published fiction writer, biographer, and memoirist and the recipient of numerous literary awards. Her novel, *The Flood*, takes place in Topeka during the *Brown v. Board of Education* desegregation case.

Norm Fruchter is director of the Institute for Education and Social Policy at New York University. From 1983 to 1993, he was an elected member of a Brooklyn district school board, and served as president from 1989 to 1993. Between 1987 and 1995, he was program adviser for education at the Aaron Diamond Foundation, where he helped develop the Corridor Program of New York-wide cluster-school improvements and the New Vision Project that has produced almost twenty new, small secondary schools in New York. During the 1970s, he helped organize and direct an alternative high school for dropouts in Newark. He is coauthor of *Choosing Equality: The Case for Democratic Schooling*, which won the American Library Association's Oboler Prize for Intellectual Freedom, and *New Directions in Parent Involvement*. He is also the author of two novels and the director of several documentary films.

Robert Berne is vice president for academic development at New York University, where he has been on the faculty since 1976. Previously, he was the dean of NYU's Robert F. Wagner Graduate School of Public Service and codirector of the Institute for Education and Social Policy. He has written extensively on education finance and governance and is coauthor of *The Measurement of Equity in School Finance* and coeditor of *Outcome Equity in Education*. In the field of public sector financial management, he has coauthored *The Financial Analysis of Governments* and authored *The Relationships between Financial Reporting and the Measurement of Financial Condition*. His work has appeared in numerous journals; he has directed several state commissions and testified in school finance court cases.